G000154822

THE ANOINTING

PASTOR:
ANNE SIMPSON-PHILLIPSON

Sunesis Publications

The Anointing

ISBN: 978-0-9928495-1-1

SUNESIS PUBLICATIONS

For more information, please visit:

WWW.STUARTPATTICO.COM

CONTENTS

INTRODUCTION

Acts 1 v 8 "You shall receive power when the Holy Spirit comes upon you and you shall be my witnesses"

The Lord has promised that a great outpouring of the Holy Spirit shall come upon us for the purpose of witnessing to the world concerning the gospel. On the day of Pentecost the disciples were waiting patiently in the upper room for the promised Holy Spirit, when suddenly there was a sound like a mighty rushing wind that began to fill the room. Tongues of fire came and separated and sat on each one of them and they began to speak in other tongues as the Spirit enabled them. The result of this was that Peter got up in the market place and began to preach the gospel of salvation and 3,000 people got saved that day.

When the power of God moves, then it will cause a reaction to happen in those who are witnessing the event. I believe that we need the Anointing of the Holy Spirit in order to be able to fulfil the call of God upon our lives and to reach the people that God wants us to reach in this world.

Isaiah 61 v 1 "The Spirit of the sovereign Lord is upon me because he has anointed me to preach good news". The Anointing is always for a reason. As we go through this book we will see the purposes that God has for our lives and how the anointing will enable us to fulfil them.

<u>What is the anointing?</u>

To anoint simply means - to smear all over with the presence of God. If you remember in the bible there was another time when Peter moved with the power of God on his life. In fact there was so much of the presence of God on his life, that even his shadow healed the sick!

Acts 5 v 15 "As a result people brought the sick into the streets and laid them on beds and mats so that at least Peter's shadow might fall on them as he passed by"

The people were so aware of the power of God on Peter's life, that they believed that even if his shadow touched them, then they would be healed. When Jesus walked on the earth, many people reached out to just touch him and they were healed instantly.

Recently I have begun to see people in meetings being healed just by the presence of God that is present. Sometimes I have not even needed to lay hands on them, but as God's presence is flowing, they have been getting healed. This is something that I have always believed should and could happen; when God is present then anything can happen. At one time in India recently as we were preparing to leave the crusade; the people were running after us begging us to lay our hands on them so that they might be healed. People are crying out for the true power of God; people are hungry to receive when they see the anointing.

After the resurrection, Jesus told his disciples that he was going to go back to his Father in heaven, but he would not leave them alone. He promised to send the Holy Spirit who would enable them to carry on the work of spreading the gospel with signs following. The Holy Spirit is now here on earth equipping and empowering us to do the work of God in the earth. I believe that we are living in times now where we can not presume to preach the gospel unless we have signs following; many are looking for evidence of who God is. There are many around the world who are hungry for the real God and yet there are so many "gods" in this world that some people are confused. When they find the true God; they will follow him with all their heart. I have witnessed that God is pouring out his Spirit in a greater way than ever before and I believe that this will increase as we approach the return of the Lord. The church will be raptured at her most glorious point in the whole of history. The world may be getting darker but God said that as the world gets darker, so the glory on the church would be greater (Isaiah 60 v 1)

John 14 v 12 "I tell you the truth, anyone who has faith in me will do what I have been doing. He will do greater things than these because I am going to the Father"

Many of us find it hard to accept, that we can even do the same things that Jesus did while he was on earth let alone do greater things! How on earth could we do greater things than Jesus did? I believe that the answer is because the Holy Spirit has been poured out on all believers now. In the Old Testament, the Holy Spirit just came upon certain believers at certain times for certain tasks, but was never available to everyone. After Jesus had ascended back into heaven, the Holy Spirit came to earth and is ready to fill every believer who asks him to. Also, although Jesus walked in power and authority while on earth, he had not yet gone to the cross and rose again and defeated death. Therefore we now proclaim an even greater message to the world, that death has been defeated and that in Jesus, we do not need to die. We will die in the natural, but spiritually we can live forever because of Jesus' victory at the cross. Every believer has now been given power and authority because of the cross.

There is also something else that we can do as Christians that Jesus could not do. We have a testimony of changed lives. Jesus could not speak to someone about how his life had been radically changed by the power of God. He could not tell someone of how he had been set free from alcohol or drug abuse, or how he had been set free from various fears in his life. We have the ability to give a testimony of what God has done in our lives and I believe that our testimonies are powerful. People may want to argue with us about the validity of the word of God, but they can not argue about what has happened to us personally. Many times after a meeting, I will invite people to come forward and give a testimony of what God has done for them in that meeting because it is an encouragement to the other people listening. It builds faith in the other people, but it also seals the work in that persons life as well, as they are declaring the works of the Lord in their own life. Often the devil wants to steal away the blessings that we have received but when we testify to God's goodness then we are confirming and holding on to the blessing that we have received. In Revelation

12 v 11 it says that "they overcame him by the blood of the Lamb and the word of their testimony". It is through the blood of the Jesus at the cross that we are saved, healed and delivered but it is also by the word of our testimony as we acknowledge the work of the cross that we fully overcome the enemy in our lives. In Romans 10 v 9 it says that if we confess with our mouth and believe in our heart, then we will be saved. When we truly believe that God has done something for us, then we need to not only believe it but we need to confess it out of our mouths as the word of our testimony becomes very powerful to those who are listening.

The anointing will enable us to be witnesses, to be able to share what God has done in our lives and will also enable us to move in the dynamic power of God. I love the anointing of God because I know that most of the things that I have been called to do; I would not be able to do in my natural personality. The anointing does not change your personality, but the anointing gives you what you need for the time that you need it. The anointing takes you out of your natural ability and into supernatural ability. As you begin to move in the anointing, you will be amazed at the things that God will do through you. I remember once when I was doing a recording for a television broadcast and as I looked at the cameras around the room, I knew that I was out of my depth in my natural abilities BUT then when I invited the Holy Spirit into the situation; suddenly the anointing came upon me and I was able to complete the broadcast with ease. When we understand the anointing, we will walk in more confidence in our lives because we will begin to realise that we are simply vessels used by God to fulfil his purposes. Every time that I get up to preach, I always ask that the Holy Spirit would speak through me and sometimes I am even amazed at what comes out of my mouth, but I have to trust that if I have asked God to speak through me, then he is speaking and that whatever I am saying, must be what people need to hear at that time. I may not know the needs of the people in a meeting, but the Holy Spirit knows each person intimately and he knows what they need to hear and receive that day. That is why it is so important that we depend upon the Holy Spirit so that people will receive what they need to receive at any given time. I remember when I first started preaching that I said to the Lord that I was not interested in just preaching nice stories if they had no relevance for the peoples lives today. I wanted to preach things that would change people's lives. We can only do this through the power of the Holy Spirit and the anointing. Often people will say to me "How did you know what I was thinking this morning?" because I had preached something that related to how they were feeling at that time. Of course, I did not know what they were thinking that morning, but the Holy Spirit did! and he wanted to let them know that he knew about their situation and that he was in control of it. That is why we need to ask the Holy Spirit to speak through us or else people will just get some nice stories but with no life and no revelation. What we need to preach is not more knowledge but more revelation knowledge; i.e.; how does this apply to peoples lives now.

Throughout this book we will look in more detail concerning what the anointing is and what the anointing does and also how we can receive and move in the anointing in our own lives.

CHAPTER 1

THE ANOINTING

We may ask ourselves; What is the anointing? What will the anointing do in my life and ministry? What difference will having the anointing make to my life?

The anointing is simply the power and the presence of God on our lives to be able to fulfil what God wants us to do. Often when people speak about the anointing, we think of some strange, mystical power that we are unable to understand, but God wants us to understand the anointing and to operate in it. The anointing will make a world of difference to everything that we do. In my own life and ministry, I have seen that the anointing enables everything to flow more easily without striving.

Zechariah 4 v 6 "not by power, nor by might, but by my Spirit says the Lord"

No longer do I get up to preach and struggle for words to say, but once the anointing is moving upon me, then words just flow out of my mouth, without me even thinking about it. The anointing seems to by-pass the intellect and brings things out from your spirit. I don't believe though, that the anointing is an excuse for not having to study or prepare or learn etc. The Holy Spirit will bring to remembrance those things which the Lord has spoken to us (John 14 v 26). So what I believe happens; is that over the years we have filled our spirits with the word of God and the things that God has done in our lives and so when we get up to minister under the power of the anointing, all of what has been stored up in our hearts, just begins to pour out of us. When we spend time in the presence of God, then everything will become easier because our time of ministry will be an overflow out of the time that we have spent in the presence of God. When we spend time with the Lord, then we begin to be filled with the presence of God and somewhere down the line, when we are so full, an overflow will take place. I believe that the anointing causes an overflow to take place, but there needs to be something within us already in order for it to overflow! If we never spend time in the presence of God or in reading his word, then we can not expect a sudden anointing of overflow to take place when we want to minister because it will not happen because there is nothing in us for God to bring out. But if we have an abundance stored up, then the anointing will begin to stir that and suddenly a gush of living water will pour forth out of our lives and into the lives of those who we are ministering to.

I have noticed that the anointing can operate in many different ways. Sometimes, when I sense the anointing upon my life, it is very quiet, but at other times, it can be very loud and bold and at times, the anointing can be so strong that you can not do anything. When I was in America recently, the anointing of God was suddenly so strong in the meeting, that people were literally laying on their faces before God and I realised that I would be unable to preach in that situation. I therefore, just prayed for the people to be filled to overflowing with the Holy Spirit and the meeting turned into a time of soaking in the presence of God instead of me preaching. When people are in the real presence of God, no human words are needed - his presence is all we need. I have always believed that if we could just bring people into the real presence of God, then all their needs would be met in that place. However on another occasion at a conference recently, I suddenly sensed the presence of God so strongly that I knew that I needed to pray for people to receive the anointing even though it was not the official time for ministry. Do you realise that God does not have an official time for ministry? We have our plans all nicely worked out for our services and we tell God when he is able to move! But God loves to move when he chooses to move and we have to be ready to move with him or else we will miss the awesome blessings that he wants to pour out. We think that we have to have worship, the word and then ministry! But on this occasion, God spoke to me half way through the worship, to get up and to invite people to come forward to receive the double anointing and the anointing was so strong that I knew that if I did not move at that exact moment, then we would lose that moment forever. As I gave the invitation, nearly everyone in the building came forward and God moved in a powerful way with lots of people also receiving the joy of the Lord in holy laughter as well as receiving the anointing for ministry. Therefore it is important to understand the moving of the Holy Spirit and the anointing because God will not fit into our little boxes and our set times.

On another time India recently, I suddenly began to sense in my spirit that the Lord wanted to set people free from fear - as I began to ask the people who wanted to be set free from fear, a lot of people put their hands up. I then invited them to come forward and I began to pray that the anointing would break every bondage in their lives - the anointing at that point was so strong and many testified with tears in their eyes that fear had left their lives - this was again all before the official preaching and ministry time! On another occasion I was in a meeting and during the worship time, I was looking at a certain lady in the congregation who had hearing aids in and the Lord said to me "I am going to heal her today". As soon as the worship had ended and I got up to speak, I immediately called that lady forward and told her that God was going to heal her that day. Let me tell you that the anointing will give you boldness because now the whole congregation is looking at me to see what God is going to do. Sometimes we want to pray quietly out the back with someone so that if nothing happens, then we won't feel embarrassed! But here I was in front of everyone declaring that God was going to do a miracle. Anyway as I prayed and put my hands on her ears, God opened her ears and she was able to hear. After that I noticed that there was more attentiveness to the message. In Acts 8 v 6 it says that when they saw the miraculous signs that Philip did, they paid close attention to what he said". It takes boldness to step out, but I have noticed that when I step out, God backs me up. We may not always receive the answer every time that we want but every step of faith lifts us to a new level and if we are following and being prompted by the Spirit of God then we are just responding to what he has already decided to do anyway. That is why we need to flow with the Holy Spirit and not just out of presumption. God is not obliged to confirm our presumptions but he will confirm his leadings. The more that we see God move, then our faith is lifted to expect more each time. Now if someone comes forward with a particular healing need and it is one that I have seen healed recently then I think "oh that is easy, saw that last week"! I believe that we should never be satisfied and always looking for more. Even though I am seeing more now than at any other time in my ministry, I know that I have not yet arrived. Another time in India I was brought a girl to pray for who was born blind and although I prayed all the right things; she still could not see when I left. When I got back to the hotel, I was asking the Lord about this because I reasoned that if Jesus had been there in the flesh then that girl would have left being able to see. I do not believe that the blockages are ever with God as he has done everything on the cross; so we must always be looking to see "Lord what do I need to do differently to see the results that you paid for on the cross?". I believe that the greatest key is the amount of time that we spend in the presence of God. I also want to mention something though to encourage some people who may be feeling that they are doing everything that they know to do and yet they are not seeing the results that they want.

Right from the time that God called me into ministry, I have always sought for the presence of God and I have always believed that the things that Jesus did and the things that the apostles did, were still available to us today and should be happening through the church and through our lives. So, I always prayed for the anointing to increase, to be able to see more miracles, to see more people responding to the gospel. For the first few years of my ministry, although I knew the anointing and the presence of God, there did not seem to be a lot of fruit taking place; although some people were healed, it was not on the scale that I wanted. There were many times when I wanted to just give up but God had given me a vision. I believe that God gives us visions because they not only direct us in the way that we should go but they also hold us firm during the dry and difficult times. Every time I wanted to give up, I would be reminded of the vision that I had seen of greater things and so I continued on. I believe that all that I am doing and seeing now was birthed in those early years when the Holy Spirit was revealing himself to me and every day I would sit and soak in his presence and read the word. I was filling myself up so that at the appointed time, the overflow would eventually take place. Then one day, I was in a meeting and the glory of God began to fill the room and suddenly all over the room, people began getting healed. I left that meeting so excited because I knew that this was what should be happening, I was also excited because I saw it first in England. Many people want to tell you that miracles only happen in other countries but my experience is that although I have seen miracles abroad, I have also seen as many miracles in my own country. I have always reasoned that God does not change because we get on an airplane; nor does the anointing on my life change either. The only difference is peoples expectation levels. If we are in a meeting where the people are open and ready to receive, then God will move in any country of the world, he is no respecter of persons or nations! So from that meeting, I knew that a breakthrough had taken place and after that I began to see that in nearly every meeting, people would get healed. Then people began to ask me "what did you do differently suddenly"? and my answer was "Nothing". God had just decided to move and breakthrough. Therefore I want to encourage you to never give up and to keep doing the works of God even during dry times, because eventually you will breakthrough. Some times we think that miracles are only for the super men and women of God but they are for every believer that will press into God and believe for them. Mark 16 v 17-18 says that for those who believe "they shall lay hands on sick people and they will get well". It doesn't say just the apostles or the pastors, it says believers. If you are a believer in Jesus then you can lay hands on sick people and see them get healed.

I also believe that we only know a small fraction of what is actually taking place and sometimes we might believe that nothing is happening when actually it is. I was in a meeting recently and a lady came up to me to tell me about a miracle that had happened 12 years ago. Apparently at the time, her daughter was expecting a baby and the baby was shown on the scan that it would be born with a deformity. At the time, I prayed over a prayer cloth and she took the cloth to her daughter. The baby was born perfectly normal with no deformity and is now a gymnast! But I knew nothing of this miracle until 12 years later. Therefore let us not become weary in doing good for we shall reap a harvest if we do not give up (Galatians 6 v 9). I believe that we may never know the extent of all that we have achieved until one day we stand before the Lord and he shows us all things. When we get to heaven, we may find that we have people coming up to us and thanking us for what we did in their lives on earth and some of those people we may not even know who they are but something that we did affected their lives for eternity. Many times when we are doing open air crusades in the nations, we may never know how many people are listening to the gospel message and responding in their lives. Only eternity will reveal the results - let us therefore be faithful in all that God has asked us to do believing that our work for the Lord is not in vain and nothing that we do for God will ever return void. Even if it seems like nothing is happening, if we are doing God's will, then something is always happening.

Even in the natural sense, some things take longer to grow than others - there are some seeds that you grow in the ground and they spring up quickly but then there are others that take a longer time. It is the same with the spiritual things that we are sowing into peoples lives. Some people we pray for them for a life time before we see any results and we may become weary and think that no change will ever happen and then others, we pray for them and see almost an overnight change. We also need to realise that often we are all links in the chain and if we receive an overnight success then often we are reaping where someone else has done the hard work before us.

I believe that the greatest key to the anointing is the time that you spend with the Lord in his presence. I always try according to my schedule to take time in the morning to just sit with the Lord and the word meditating and thinking on his goodness and what he wants to say to me that day. As we take time to spend in his presence then I believe that the anointing will be an overflow of that place. Sometimes people want me to lay hands on them to receive the anointing which I often do but I also believe that you will only maintain the anointing through the depth of your relationship.

WHAT WILL THE ANOINTING DO?

There is so much that the anointing will do, but I want to list 9 things that I believe the anointing will do in our lives. It is interesting that there are 9 fruits of the spirit and 9 gifts of the Holy Spirit and so now I want us to look at 9 main things that the anointing will do in our lives.

1) The anointing will open your spiritual eyes and give you vision

Revelation 3 v 18 "anoint thine eyes that thou may see" (KJV)

The anointing of God upon your life will open your spiritual eyes; so that you can see what the Lord wants you to see. Suddenly you will begin to see situations how God sees them instead of through your natural understanding.

In 2 Kings 6 we read the story where Elisha and his servant were surrounded by the enemy, but then as the servant begins to panic, Elisha prays:-

V17 "Oh Lord, open his eyes that he may see. Then the Lord opened the servant's eyes, and he looked and saw the hills full of horses and chariots of fire all around Elisha"

In the natural it looked like a dangerous situation, but when the servants' eyes were opened to see into the spiritual realm, he then realised that they were not alone, but God had sent a multitude of angels to surround them and that they were safe. I

19

believe that if God was to open our spiritual eyes for just a minute, we would be totally amazed by what we would see. Most of the time, God does not allow us to see things like that because we might not be able to handle what we would see. However, I believe that we are surrounded by angels all the time and especially when we are in times of danger. I also believe that our lives may have been saved many times without us even realising it, because angels do not usually make themselves known, they work behind the scenes on our behalf under the instruction of God. There was a situation once when I was in Kenya and we were staying in some accommodation up a flight of stairs. As I reached the top of the stairs, I missed one of the steps and tripped. As I tripped, I let out a scream and also threw my mobile phone up in the air. I was watching as my mobile phone was about to go over the railings and crash to the ground below and I was thinking "Oh No, there goes my phone!" As I was thinking this; suddenly my phone came back and landed on the floor in front of me! And now I was wondering "how on earth did that happen!". I believe that angels caught my phone and threw it back. Not only was I pleased to get my phone back, but it was also re-assuring to know that angels were all around us in that place.

Hebrews 1 v 14 "Are not all angels ministering spirits sent to serve those who will inherit salvation"

Angels are sent by God to minister to us! I believe that operating under the anointing also activates angels to work on our behalf. I believe that when we are in a meeting and the anointing of God is present, there are also angels in that

20

meeting. Isaiah 63 v 9 speaks about "the angel of his presence". There have been many times, when even in a small group of people meeting for worship, it has sounded as though there were hundreds of people singing. I have often thought that angels have come to join us for worship! If God opened our eyes, we would be amazed.

Although God may not literally open our eyes to see into the spiritual realm, he does open our spiritual eyes to see spiritual truths and also to receive revelation and vision concerning the things that he wants us to do. The Holy Spirit is the one who shines a light on the word of God and makes it come alive to us. We may be reading the word and suddenly a scripture jumps out at us and becomes alive and takes on a whole new meaning that we had never seen before. The Holy Spirit will give us revelation concerning our lives and the things that he is planning for us. He loves to reveal his will for our lives so that we can work with him to fulfil it.

We may be praying and suddenly we receive a desire to do something or we may have a dream or see a picture of something. God chooses many different ways to speak to us, but he does desire to speak to us and to communicate the will of God for our lives.

In Acts 16 Paul wanted to go to Bithynia to preach the gospel, but the Holy Spirit would not allow him to go there. Instead he had a dream in the night of a man from Macedonia begging him to come and preach there. He therefore, concluded that he should go to Macedonia. The Holy Spirit redirected his plans and showed him the direction that he wanted him to go in. The Lord can communicate to us in many different ways, but the anointing will bring direction and vision into our lives.

The anointing will enable us to be able to believe for things that in the natural may look impossible, but with God all things are impossible. A friend of mine, who I sometimes stay with when I travel, has a little sign that says; "dream your dreams, a size too big, so that you can grow into them". If your dream is manageable in your own strength, then it probably did not come from God. Dreams from God will often leave you wondering how on earth you are going to achieve them or how you are going to get there. That does not mean that we are to dream fantasies! There is a difference between living our lives in fantasy land, and living our lives dreaming God dreams. We need to look to see if there is any evidence of what God has said. In other words, even if we do not see anywhere near what God has shown us yet, is there any evidence that it may at least be possible in the future? In other words, if you believe that you will have a big preaching ministry and you see yourself standing in front of thousands of people, maybe you could ask yourself this:- Even if you are not experiencing this now - do you at least know that you are anointed to preach? When you preach, do you and others recognise an anointing on you to do so? Do you seem to operate in the gifts that would indicate that a bigger ministry is ahead for you? When you preach, even if only to a few people, do you see things happen, do people get challenged, healed, delivered when you minister? Do people get saved when you preach the gospel even if it is only a few? Is God asking you to do things that would indicate an enlargement is on the way? For example, when the Lord began to speak to me about writing more books, I knew that he was preparing me for enlargement. God would not ask me to write more books if he wasn't going to give me more places to take them to. He also took me through a season where he began to reveal to me that it was time to prepare and get more organised because enlargement was on the way. Recently the Lord has also began to prepare me for a TV ministry which is another enlargement on the ministry. We may go through different seasons and one of those seasons is different times of preparation. If we do not understand seasons, then we can sometimes get frustrated and think that nothing is happening. However, when God is at work, something is always happening, even if un-seen. Often the times of preparation are preparing us for a greater move ahead.

The anointing will give us vision and the anointing will also birth those visions within our hearts. We need to hold on to the things that God has spoken into our lives, for if they are truly of God, then they will surely come to pass. God promises in his word that what he has spoken; he will fulfil because he is not a man that he should lie (Numbers 23 v 19). Sometimes, we may wonder - how can I know if a desire has truly come from God? I believe that if the desire is a godly desire that will not go away even when you have been tested and tried, then it is very likely to be a God desire. Our own desires tend to change quite quickly when testing comes along or when something better shows up. However, desires from God will stay with you no matter what you may go through - in fact they can even increase through difficult times. Often a vision from God will also be confirmed by another witness through the form of a prophetic word giving us encouragement that we are hearing from the Lord and walking on the right path way. Let us not become weary for every vision shall be established at the proper time if we do not give up.

The anointing will open your spiritual eyes.

Ephesians 1 v 18 "I pray also that the eyes of your heart may be enlightened in order that you may know the hope to which he has called you"

Our spiritual eyes are in our heart, not in our face! God wants to open up the eyes in our hearts to know him more and to understand the things that he has for our lives.

2) The anointing will change your attitude

1 Samuel 10 v 9 - "As Saul turned to leave, God changed his heart"

After Saul had received the anointing from Samuel to become the next king, it says that God changed his heart. He then found a company of prophets and he began to prophesy because of the anointing that was on him. As we will see later in the book, Saul lost his anointing because of disobedience, but at this time, his heart was turned towards God.

Ecclesiastics 9 v 8 - "anoint your head with oil"

The anointing will change our attitudes and begin to give us the mind of Christ.

1 Corinthians 2 v 16 "but we have the mind of Christ"

A lot of the battles that we go through, start off in our minds. If we dwell upon something for long enough, then in the end, we will want to do the thing that we have been thinking about, either good or bad. We need to ask the Lord to anoint our head, our minds, so that we will have the right attitudes and thoughts in our minds. I believe that this is one area that is the hardest to conquer because the mind is the battlefield. This is the area where the enemy tries to put thoughts of temptations and fears and doubts and if we dwell upon them, then they can begin to destroy our lives.

James 1 v 14-15 "each one is tempted, when by his own evil desires, he is dragged away and enticed. Then after desire has conceived, it gives birth to sin, and sin when it is full grown gives birth to death"

So we see that there is a progression of sin that takes place, but it begins with the temptation in our minds to do something. We can not help the thoughts that come into our minds, but we can help what we do with them after that.

2 Corinthians 10 v 5 "we take captive every thought to make it obedient to Christ"

In other words, if those thoughts would not lead to actions that would glorify God, then we need to take a hold of them and cast them down. We need to bring them in line with the word of God and take authority over them, and refuse to dwell on them any longer. The anointing will cleanse us and purify us and help us to think upon those things which are pure and holy.

3) <u>The anointing will give you power to overcome the enemy</u>

In 1 Samuel 17, we read the story of David and Goliath and how David overcame the giant because of the anointing that was upon his life. There may be many giants that we will face in our lives, but the anointing has the power to overcome all of them. All the Israelites were afraid of Goliath and no-one wanted to go and fight against him. He had brought terror to the Israelite camp until one day a little shepherd boy called David came along to the battle line. In the previous chapter, David had been anointed by Samuel to be the next king, so he knew that the anointing of God was upon his life. Despite all the attempts of the people to deter David from going into the battle, David was determined to go and fight against Goliath. Goliath began to mock him and try to intimidate him, but David stood in the power and authority of the anointing upon his life. While Goliath went out to the battle with armour and spears and javelins, David simply went out dressed as a shepherd boy with no armour on and just a sling and a stone. No wonder, Goliath mocked him; in the natural it looked ridiculous, but David had something that Goliath did not have - he had the anointing of God! and as David slung that stone, it killed Goliath outright!! God knows how to aim properly!

The anointing has the power to overcome the enemy, to destroy giants in our lives and to bring victory. David then went over to Goliath and took his own sword from him and cut off his head with it. This was the sword that Goliath had boasted he would kill David with but it was turned back on him because of the anointing. For some of you, the enemy may have tried to bring all kinds of trials and difficulties into your life, but God can turn those things around if you will hand them over to him. The things that the enemy sent to destroy you, can actually take you to your destiny. No matter what we may have gone through, the anointing can turn those situations around. What the devil meant for harm, God can use for good. What we have been through can be used as a powerful weapon in the hands of God. When we come through victorious, then our testimony is powerful for setting others free.

God can make a way where there seems to be no way. We may have felt that we could not serve God because of obstacles and circumstances, but God is the one who parted the red sea so that the Israelites could go through on dry ground. He is the same God who will part the sea and make a way for you.

4) <u>You will move in the dynamic</u>

Acts 3 v 8 "silver or gold we do not have, but what we have we give you, in the name of Jesus Christ of Nazareth, walk"

What do we have?? The man who sat at the entrance to the temple was begging for money because he was lame and needed money because he was unable to work. There was no social security in those days and he needed to beg for money to survive. When Peter and John saw him, they saw that his greatest need was not for money, but was to be healed, so that he didn't need to beg any more. If they had given him money, he would still have been back the next day for more, but if he was healed, he would be able to support himself and not need to keep coming back to beg for more money. Peter and John had received the anointing and knew that they had the power to command the man to get up and walk in Jesus name.

The anointing will help us to move in the dynamic and to see signs and wonders when we pray. Jesus called his disciples to go and preach the gospel and to heal the sick, raise the dead and cast out demons. He still calls us to do the same things today and it is the anointing that will enable us to be able to do it. As God has opened the nations to me, it is the anointing that enables me to see signs and wonders and it is the signs and wonders that confirm the gospel message. In many nations, when the people see God performing miracles, then they will easily respond to the gospel when they know that Jesus is real. In one town in India, we saw a man who had not been able to speak for 20 years - as we prayed for him and laid our hands on him and commanded his tongue to be loosed - he was instantly healed and came to the microphone to give his testimony. Everyone in the village knew this man; they knew that he had been mute and now he was talking. After this, many more people came to receive Jesus into their lives. To be effective in these end times, we must move in the anointing of miracles. Another man came forward in this same mission to ask me to pray for him to be healed of an injury that he had. I asked him if he knew Jesus and he said that he didn't. Then I asked him if he would like to know Jesus, to which he responded that he would just like me to pray for him to be healed. At this point, I realised that he was wanting to first know if this Jesus who I had been speaking about was real! So I prayed for him and God healed him - then after receiving his healing, he also asked to receive Jesus as his saviour. Before we went to this village, we had prayed in our hotel room and I remember saying "Lord, we can not go to this village unless you give us miracles". The Lord responded by confirming his word with signs following.

5) <u>You will have joy</u>

Psalm 45 v 7 "anointing with the oil of joy"

There is an anointing of joy which God pours out upon his people.

Psalm 16 v 11 "in his presence is fullness of joy"
If the anointing is the power and the presence of God, then it stands to reason, that there will be joy when we know and walk in the anointing of God, because there is joy in the presence of God.

I believe that there are two reasons why we will know joy when we walk in the anointing:-

First we need to realise that there is a difference between joy and happiness. Happiness is dependant upon your circumstances and therefore can change according to what is going on in your life. However, joy is a supernatural gift from the Holy Spirit and is not dependant on circumstances. We can be going through the greatest trial of our lives, and yet know joy in the midst of it.

Nehemiah 8 v 10 "the joy of the Lord is our strength".

In the midst of a trial, God may give us his joy as our strength to be able to cope and come through our circumstances. So, sometimes we will get joy because we need to have strength, but sometimes I have experienced a sense of joy for no apparent reason other than the Lord just wanting to impart that to me. Sometimes I have laid in bed at night and felt the presence of the Lord and have had a sense of excitement concerning the future come over me. Sometimes, God just wants to encourage us at different times. Also the Holy Spirit knows what is ahead for us and if he is living within us, then his excitement can flow over to us as well and although we may not know what we are excited about, we know that it is good. So, we can have a supernatural infusion of joy that is a gift from the Holy Spirit, but I believe that there is another reason why the anointing will bring joy into our lives.

If we are walking in the anointing, then we will begin to see God using us to perform miracles and change peoples lives, this will give us joy. If we go and preach the gospel and see people get saved, then we will be joyful. If we pray for someone and they get healed or set free from something, then again we have a reason to rejoice. The bible says that angels rejoice over one sinner who repents. I was once preaching in a prison, where lots of men had put their hands up to receive Jesus as their saviour and as I turned to my right, I sensed in my spirit, a circle of angels, who were holding hands and jumping up and down. I truly believe that the Lord allowed me to see a glimpse that day of the angels rejoicing over the salvations that were taking place. If angels rejoice, then I believe that we too can rejoice when God uses us to bring others into his Kingdom. I certainly remember that day coming away feeling very joyful at what I had just seen take place. Therefore walking in the anointing will cause us to have joy because we will see amazing things happening.

After we returned from the mission in India where we had seen the mute speak and the deaf hear and eye sight being restored and many people giving their lives to the Lord there was a joy in my heart as I laid in my bed that night. Sometimes ministering in some nations can have challenges. On this particular occasion; we had not been able to get our bed sheets back because it had been raining and the hotel had not been able to get them dry! But I remember laying on my bed and thinking "well Lord, today we saw the mute speak, the deaf hear and all kind of others being healed! What does it matter, if we don't have bed sheets"!! The joy of the Lord begins to put all other things that we would normally moan about into perspective.

6) <u>The anointing will change your appearance and your speech</u>

Acts 4 v 13 "they took note that they had been with Jesus"
V20 "We can not help speaking about what we have seen and heard"

31

The people realised that the apostles were ordinary, un-schooled men and yet they took note that they had been with Jesus. In other words, there was nothing remarkable about them in the natural sense, they were ordinary men but there was something about them that made them stand out - they had been with Jesus. But, how did they know that they had been with Jesus?

I believe that when we have spent time with Jesus, there will be something about us that will look different, even if people don't know what it is. When Moses went up the mountain for 40 days, the bible says, that his face shone when he came down. Being in the presence of God has the ability to bring radiance to our faces and also to make us look younger. God said that he would renew our youth, and there is something about being in the presence of God, that makes us look younger. I often joke, that we don't need any anti-age wrinkling creams; we just need more of the presence of God on our lives! Sometimes, you might meet people who have lived their lives without God and suffered many stresses and strains in their lives and they appear to be about 10-20 years older than they actually are. We may then meet someone, who although they may still have gone through difficulties, they have lived their lives with God and there is a radiance about them. They can often look 10-20 years younger than they actually are, because God has re-vitalised them and kept them looking young. In fact I often meet people who I have not seen for many years and they often tell me that I don't look any older than when they knew me before and want to know what my secret is! The secret is being in the presence of God who renews our youth.

I believe that we can also tell a lot about someone by looking in their eyes - they say, that they are the gateway to the soul. The Lord wants to put a sparkle in our eyes, to make us look alive, that others may see life and hope in us.

When we spend time with the Lord, not only will our appearance change, but so will our speech. You can tell a lot about someone by the things that they talk about. If you listen to some conversations, it can be quite sad to hear the trivial things that people talk about as if there is no real meaning to their lives. Not only will the Lord give us a more pure speech than before we knew him, but the things that we will want to talk about will change. That is why it is so good to have regular fellowship with others who want to talk about the same things that we want to talk about. It encourages us and it lifts us up when we are able to meet with like minded people to talk about the Lord and what he is doing in our lives.

When the anointing is on our lives, we will also be able to speak about the gospel more clearly. When the apostles were being threatened not to speak about Jesus, they responded by saying, we can not help but speak about him. In other words, he has changed our lives so much, that we can not keep silent about him, we must preach the gospel.

7) <u>The anointing will change your position</u>

The anointing will promote you to a higher place of influence. In

Acts 6 we read about a man called Stephen who was chosen to be a deacon to wait on tables. The bible says that he was a man full of the Holy Spirit and faith and so he was chosen for the position of being a deacon. However, a few lines down, we read that a promotion has taken place. This same man is now operating as an evangelist and performing many miracles among the people. He had a promotion because of the anointing but also because of his faithfulness in a lower position.

No matter what we have been called to do, God will always start us off in a smaller position, not only to train us and prepare us, but also to see what our attitude will be like in that place. When we have been faithful with small things, then God will promote us and give us a higher position. When you are faithful and moving in the anointing, you can not stay in a low place for long - God will lift you up.

After God first gave me the vision that he wanted me to preach; I did not immediately start in that position but I began by using the skills that God had given to me to serve a local pastor. I would work in the church office as a volunteer and type letters and make cups of coffee and then distribute church leaflets around the local houses. Then slowly I was asked to take on more responsibility and to lead the evangelism team and eventually I ended up planting a church and establishing my own itinerant ministry where today I not only travel around the UK but to many nations of the world. But it began by being faithful with small things and then God changes your position and promotes you to a higher place. I believe that this takes place not only in the natural but also in the spiritual. When God realises that he can trust us, then he also begins to reveal more spiritual truths to us as well. He longs to share his heart with us but is also wanting to know who he can trust. Let us be people who will be faithful in the ways of the Lord.

8) Persecution and Protection

We need to also realise though that the anointing of God on your life will not attract everyone. To those who are hungry for God, they will be attracted to you, but to those who are trying to avoid God or those who are religious people, they will be irritated by you. The power of God will always cause a reaction. Jesus caused reactions wherever he went. Some people loved him and ran to everywhere he was, but others wanted to kill him and some even asked him to leave their towns. When we walk with the anointing on our life, we will at times be misunderstood, and at times be openly persecuted, but the anointing will also bring divine protection from God.

Psalm 20 v 6 "God saves his anointed"
Psalm 18 v 50 "He shows un-failing kindness to his anointed"

God commands that we should not touch his anointed men and women because he will stand on their behalf. Sometimes even in the church, we can be guilty of coming against God's anointed people and we need to be very careful. God will not stand for people coming against his chosen and anointed people, and when we set ourselves up in this position, we can place ourselves in a dangerous position before God. We may not always understand how someone operates in a certain ministry or gift but we need to be very careful when we begin to moan and complain and criticise those who are trying to serve God. We are all human and even ministers will make mistakes, but we are called to support and pray for our leaders, not bring them down.

After Saul had lost the presence of God, he was jealous of David and tried to kill him several times, but each time God protected David. Twice David had the opportunity to kill Saul, but he did not take the opportunity for he said "I shall not lay a hand on the Lord's anointed". Even though Saul had lost the presence of God, he still had the title of King and David would not touch him even though he was trying to kill David. He left Saul in God's hands, knowing that God would take care of the situation.

When we walk in the anointing, we may have opposition at times, but God has promised to protect us and stand on our behalf. Again that doesn't mean that we will not go through some trying times, but God will vindicate us and bring us through. In the bible many prophets and apostles went through horrendous things because of the anointing on their lives and what they were called to do, but many times, we see God turn the situation around for good. For example, when Paul and Silas were in prison for preaching the gospel, they were given supernatural joy to be able to praise God even in the prison, and as they began to praise God, the whole prison was shaken and everyone's chains came off. The result was that the jailer in the prison and his whole family got saved. So even in the midst of persecution, God's power can still be at work.

9) <u>The anointing will meet our own needs</u>

Isaiah 10 v 27 KJV "The yoke shall be destroyed because of the anointing"

We often think of the anointing as something we only need if we are in ministry, but the anointing as we have seen can help us in every area of our lives. The anointing also has the ability to breakthrough and meet our own needs as well. When I minister on the anointing, I nearly always tell people to come forward for prayer all at the same time rather than queuing up for different issues; because I believe that the anointing is the power of God to meet whatever need we have. When we respond to a time of ministry, God knows what our needs are and he knows what he needs to do in our lives.

The anointing can empower us to fulfil the call of God on our lives, but the anointing can also heal us and set us free. Over the years as I have prayed for people to receive the anointing, I have seen amazing things. I have even had people wanting to get saved, while they were standing in the line for the anointing! I have seen people get healed; I have seen people getting delivered and set free. Sometimes, I receive a specific word to pray over someone, if God gives me a word of knowledge etc, but a lot of the time if I have a line of people waiting for prayer, I will just ask God to release the anointing and then pray over each person for the anointing to come and watch as God does whatever he wants to do in each person's life. When the anointing touches people's lives, everyone will react differently. For some there will seem to be little reaction (this doesn't mean nothing is happening). For others, they may be slain in the spirit and rest in the Lord, for others they may cry or shake, others may scream or make other more noticeable reactions such as in deliverance. I have also noticed that demons do not like the anointing; this is often when someone will scream or begin to shake violently or even be thrown backwards. Often the Lord will instruct me to pray for the fire of God to come upon people as well.

Mathew 3 v 11 "he will baptise with the Holy Spirit and with fire"

The fire of God is connected with the anointing and again there can be two aspects to fire. Fire can be good or it can be destructive. When the fire of God comes upon our lives, it can be to empower us, to set us on fire for God, to give us a greater passion for the things of God. But fire will also burn up anything within us that is not of God; fire can be a purifying thing as well. I remember once, I was in a meeting in Scotland and the Lord had instructed me to pray for the fire of God to come upon certain people in the meeting. The meeting though was being held in a hotel function room. When you are under the anointing, you often forget about where you are and it was only after I had shouted "FIRE" for about the tenth time and the waiters began to appear from out of the kitchen, that I suddenly realised that maybe I should not be shouting FIRE so loudly!!!! It is a bit of a standing joke now amongst those who know me, that if we hold a meeting in a hotel, that we need to be careful about not shouting FIRE! At one point, I was even nick-named the fire lady! I am sure that the Lord has a sense of humour - he must have to work with us!

So the anointing can meet the needs within our own lives and I have seen the anointing touch people and change lives everywhere I go. It is so exciting to walk in the anointing and see what he does in people's lives. Sometimes we don't always hear the results of all that we do, but at times when we need to be encouraged the Lord provides it for us. A while back, I was feeling a bit low because of various situations and I went to do a meeting in the north of England. When I got there, a lady who I had prayed for in the past came up to me, to let me know what happened the last time I had prayed for her. She had been waiting to have an operation to remove a tumour and had come forward for prayer. When I prayed for her, she believed that she had been healed, but still went along to the hospital the next day anyway. When she got there, they did some tests to find out exactly where the tumour was, but they couldn't find one!!! It had completely disappeared - hallelujah!! When we hear things like this, it makes everything worthwhile. Serving God and walking in the anointing is the most amazing thing that we can do with our lives. To see people's lives changed by the power of God is an awesome privilege.

CHAPTER 2

DAVID'S ANOINTING – GIANT DESTROYING ANOINTING

The story of David is such an encouragement to us, as we often feel that we would not be chosen to be anointed. David however, was overlooked by his own family, but was chosen by God to become King. When God called David, he was just a young shepherd boy out in the field tending his sheep, he didn't even come into the house when Samuel called to anoint one of the sons of Jesse to be the next King, but God knew where David was and would not let Samuel leave until he had found him.

God knows where you are? We may feel that God has overlooked us, that we are just in the background not being noticed, but God has noticed us and when the time is ready, he will call us. Be faithful where God has placed at this time and if God wants to promote you, he will call you at the appropriate time.

1 Samuel 16 v 7 "Man looks at the outward appearance, but God looks at the heart"

All of the Sons of Jesse came in to stand in front of Samuel and they were all handsome and strong and in the natural Samuel thought to himself, "surely, the Lord's anointed stands here" but God said "No, I have rejected all of them". Samuel was looking with his natural eyes, but God was looking at the heart. He knew that although they may have had the outward

41

qualifications, they did not have the right heart for the job. When Samuel asks if there are any more sons, he is told that there is David but he is tending the sheep. His family did not think that it was worthwhile Samuel seeing him, but Samuel insists on seeing him. As soon as he is brought in, the Lord instructs Samuel that he is the one and that he should anoint him. The one that was un-considered, was the one that was chosen by God. The world may have passed you by, but today God is passing by and choosing you if your heart is right towards him!

Saul, who was King at the time in name, had lost the presence of God because of his disobedience to God and he was being tormented by an evil spirit. Therefore he commands that David be brought to him to play a harp to relieve him of his torment. When David played the harp, the evil spirit left Saul. So, one of the first things that we can notice about David is that he had an anointing to worship on his life, he was a worshipper. I believe that if we want the anointing of God on our lives, we must be a worshipper above all else. No matter what we may be called to do for God, our foremost and primary calling is to worship. From that place of worship and intimacy, then everything else will flow. David also had a humility in his life - even though he knew that he had been anointed to be King, he was still willing to serve. He could have become arrogant and refused to serve Saul, taking the attitude that Saul had been rejected and that he was now chosen to take his place, so why should he serve him? He could have also been proud and thought that he was more spiritual than Saul, because he had the presence of God and Saul didn't. However, he still recognised the position that Saul had and he served him as one of his armour bearers.

In 1 Samuel 17, we read the story of David and Goliath, which we touched on earlier and we will now bring out a few more points on this story. Jesse's brothers had gone down to the battle but David went back and forth to look after the sheep.

V 15 "but David went back and forth from Saul to tend his father's sheep"

He didn't abandon his responsibilities just because he had been given a higher position. He cared about his sheep and he was faithful to look after them. He knew what God had spoken over his life for the future, but he remained faithful in the place he was at now. Some of us may have received great words over our lives for the future, but we need to be faithful with the sheep where we are now until God releases us further.

Jesse instructed David to go down to the battle line and take some supplies for his brothers, but when he gets there, he wants to know what is going on in the battle. His brothers begin to mock him and tell him to go back to his few sheep in the desert. They are jealous of him, because he was chosen to be anointed and they were not. The anointing will always cause some people to be jealous of you, but David ignores them and speaks to someone else. There was a giant of the Philistine camp called Goliath who was taunting the Israelites and daring one of them to come and fight against him. No-one was willing to go, but David begins to ask if they will allow him to go and fight. The response is that they do not believe that he is able to go, because he is only a boy and Goliath is a grown man! David however, will not be put off and when they see that he is determined to go, they allow him to go. When we have the anointing on our lives, we will have boldness to do what looks impossible in the natural. I like the way that David was not put off by the negative reactions that he got. He could have just gone back to the sheep and forgotten all about fighting Goliath but he was persistent in wanting to fight. People may often want to tell us about what we cannot do, but if God has spoken, then we need to not be put off, but to step out in faith. I believe that there is a balance between us waiting on God and God waiting on us! If we want to move forward in ministry, then although it is God who ultimately opens the doors, he does sometimes want us to push them too. We are not just to sit idly at home waiting for all the opportunities to come to us, we have to use what we have already been given and begin moving forward in faith. When Saul realised that he could not deter him from going, he tries to give him some armour to wear but David decides to take it off because he does not feel comfortable in it

V 39 "I can not go in these because I am not used to them. So he took them off"

The anointing is unique to us and although we may be able to learn from others, we can never be the same as someone else. Saul wanted David to be like him, so he dressed him in his own armour, but David did not feel comfortable and preferred instead to go with just a sling and a stone in his hand. We need to find the place that we feel comfortable with. God has made us unique and we need to allow ourselves to operate in our uniqueness; not trying to copy someone else.

As David stepped out to meet Goliath, he begins to taunt him and mock him but David knows who's authority he is standing in and he says to him:-

V45 "You come against me with sword and spear and javelin, but I come against you in the name of the Lord Almighty".

David had confidence in the anointing of God on his life and he knew that God would enable him to gain the victory. Sometimes the giants in front of us can look intimidating, but we need to stand in the power of God, knowing that one shot from God can knock that giant dead. As David aims his sling, the stone hits Goliath right in the middle of his forehead, killing him outright. After David had cut off his head with his own sword, the Israelites then move in and plunder the enemy's camp.

The anointing will remove the giants and will enable us to plunder the enemies camp. We can take back what the enemy has stolen from us. When Saul realised that Goliath was dead, he wanted to know who the young man was who had defeated him. I find this a rather strange verse because David was one of Saul's armour bearers; he played a harp for him when he was tormented by the evil spirit, so why did he not recognise who he was on the battle field? He had David brought near to him and said:-

V 58 "Whose son are you young man? Saul asked him. David said, "I am the son of your servant Jesse of Bethlehem"

Why did Saul not recognise who his own armour bearer was? Why did he not recognise the young man who played the harp to bring relief to him? I believe that the answer to this; is that Saul had only ever seen David as the young shepherd boy who played the harp nicely; he had never seen him operating under the warrior anointing. You see, the anointing can totally transform you and make you un-recognisable for the time that you are operating in it. In my natural personality, I am a quiet person, not extravert at all, but sometimes when the anointing is on me, I can become loud and bold and you would not know that it was the same person. I once went to a meeting and afterwards one lady said to me "you were not the same person that I sat next to in the car coming here". Well, I was the same person, but it was the anointing working through me that made me look like a different person just for that period of time needed. That is why anyone with a right heart who is called, can serve God because it is God's ability not yours, all he asks for is a vessel to work through. I must add that God is not always loud when he ministers; some of the most powerful meetings I have been in have in fact been very still and quiet. Often when I speak about entering into the Holy of Holies; there is a holy stillness that begins to descend upon the meeting which is awesome and beautiful. Then at other times it can be loud if we are talking about being set free etc; we just need to know how the Holy Spirit is moving in each particular situation and move with him.

I love the way that allowing God to take control can be so exciting - as I stand up to speak, I often think "Ok Lord, what way are we moving today?" Is it a gentle move of your spirit or a more bold move, where are we going today Lord?" I usually get a pretty good idea by the time I stand up as to how God wants to move in that particular service according to the atmosphere that is in the place. Is it a sensitive, intimate atmosphere or is it a breakthrough cry that is in the place? All we have to do then is to flow with what God is already doing. We need to be sensitive to how he is moving and to not quench the Holy Spirit. God will work through us, but he doesn't take us over without our permission. If God is moving in an awesome quiet way and we decide that we are going to get up and shout, then he will not stop us, but we will lose the anointing for that service and miss out on what God had intended to do. I have sometimes noticed that the anointing can be easier to lose than it is to find. When God shows up, we need to be sensitive to him and to flow in the direction that he is moving.

Saul did not recognise David because he was operating under the anointing and we too may become un-recognisable for a while, but let's allow God to work through us however he chooses to.

The next part of David's life was spent in service to Saul, but when Saul became jealous of the anointing on his life, David had to flee for his life because Saul wanted to kill him. However, in 2 Samuel 2 we see that David was anointed to be King over Judah and then in 2 Samuel 5, he was anointed to be King over the whole of Israel. All that God had prophesied years earlier came true in David's life, but he had to wait for the timing of God and had a lot of trials to go through before he finally received all that God had prepared for him.

Anointing V a Title

I believe that it is important that we realise that having the anointing of God is more important than having a title. The anointing of God, may lead you to have a title, or it may not. However, it is possible to carry a title all of our lives and yet never know the anointing or the presence of God in our lives and that is very sad. There are even some ministers who do not believe in the gospel or the fundamental truths of the Christian faith and yet they carry the title of being a minister all their lives. I remember when I first came to know the Lord; I was advised by some friends of mine, that when I went to look for a church to attend, that I should make sure that the vicar was a Christian!! At the time, I thought that this was a strange thing for someone to say, as I assumed that of course the minister would be a Christian. I have since understood what they meant though, as it is possible to think that you are serving God all your life, but never really know him. I believe that the vicars' who are in this position may be very sincere in wanting to help people, but they have never come to a revelation of God for themselves. Some people may have even gone into the ministry because it is a family heritage. So, having a title in itself does not mean that we have the anointing of God upon our lives. Unless we know God and have the anointing upon our lives, then we will never be able to lead others to a true knowledge of the Lord either. I have often said that we can only lead others as far as we have been ourselves. That is why it is so important that we get to know the Lord more closely, so that we can lead others into that place.

Saul was chosen to be King and to begin with he was anointed by God but because he began to disobey the Lord, God decided to reject him (1 Samuel 15) and chose someone else to succeed him as King, which was David as we read in the story earlier. David, who had a heart after God had the anointing of God upon his life and yet he did not yet have a title. Saul still held the title of King but had lost the presence of God to such an extent that an evil spirit began to torment him. The bible even says that the Lord had left Saul (1 Samuel 18 v 12) and was with David but nevertheless Saul still had the title but without presence.

I believe that there are two mistakes that we can make with this issue of anointing and titles:- either we assume that we are anointed because we carry a title, when in fact we may not be. Maybe we are trusting more in our title, than in knowing the presence of God. Or, we have been anointed, but we are not stepping out in faith with that anointing, because we are still waiting for someone to give us a title.

I would rather have the anointing than a title - if people want to give me titles, then that is fine, but at the end of the day, I seek to know the presence of God and to just get on with what he has called me to do. In different cultures, I have noticed that this whole area of titles is more important than others. I seem to have different titles and can operate in different ministries according to where I am. When I am at the church, then I am a pastor, but if there is a meeting where people don't know the Lord, I can operate as an evangelist. Often the Lord will give me words for the body of Christ and in some places where I go to preach, I am also advertised as a Prophet. I believe that I have many different aspects to my ministry, but at the end of the day, I am a servant of God. We may all have areas that we operate in more than others, or some of us may be able to function in all areas of ministry, but the main thing that matters is having the anointing of God upon our lives. Sometimes when we seek to give ourselves a title we can also "restrict God" because if we label ourselves then others will assume that is all that we operate in or they may put un-due pressure on us to operate in that gifting. I fully believe in the 5 fold ministry and have no problem with people having titles if they are genuinely from God but let us not seek for a title but rather seek for the anointing.

We do not need to wait until someone gives us a badge that says "evangelist" on it, before we start evangelising. If we feel that is our calling, then just step out and do it. Your calling will become evident as you begin to operate in it and then someone may begin to recognise you as an evangelist and your title may come later. Anointing always comes before a title, not the other way around. When people begin to recognise that you have an anointing in a certain area, then your title will appear.

David had received the anointing to be King a long time before he received his title. During his time of waiting, he had to prove himself faithful in the place that God had put him at that time. He also had to serve the previous King whom he would succeed even though God's presence had left the previous King, he still held the title. He had to remain strong, even when Saul wanted to kill him. Eventually David received the title that he had been anointed for all those years before.

One thing that we can also learn from this story is that David respected Saul's title, even though Saul had lost the anointing. The anointing is not supposed to make us proud and it is not so that we can ignore those who have titles. God allowed Saul to remain in place until the appointed time for David to take over, and David refused to lay a hand on him, instead believing that God would vindicate him. Saul was still the anointed of God because he had been given a specific task earlier in his life; however he had lost the anointing. I believe that there is a difference between being "anointed" and having the "anointing", although they can often go together, they do not always do so. Anointed means something that happened, but anointing is something that is still happening - a movement, a flow that is continually operating in your life. Let us not look to just be anointed but to move in the anointing! Constantly flowing in the power of God, not just relying on the fact that someone laid hands on us ten years ago and said that we were anointed for a task. Let us get into the presence of God on a regular basis and seek for the daily outpouring of the anoinTING!!

Once we have the anointing, then use it to serve God and others and God will promote you in due season.

CHAPTER 3

ELIJAH'S MANTLE AND THE DOUBLE PORTION

Elijah was a mighty Prophet of God in the Old Testament who was used to raise up another Prophet by the name of Elisha. We can see from the story of Elijah and Elisha, a spiritual principle of how to receive a double portion of the anointing in our lives.

There is so much more that the Lord wants to give to us - there is a double portion of the anointing that he desires to pour on our lives and he wants us to ask him for it so that the Kingdom of God may be extended in the earth.

Isaiah 61 v 7 "Instead of their shame, my people will receive a double portion"

We see Elijah in 1 Kings 19 being instructed by the Lord to go and find Elisha and to anoint him as the next successor to him. Elijah is to train him and mentor him so that he will become the next Prophet in the land. Elijah had just come from a testing time in his life and ministry. After confronting the prophets of Baal on Mount Carmel and seeing the fire of God fall, he is then threatened by Jezebel and has to flee for his life. How interesting that this great Prophet of God who saw fire fall from heaven and saw his prayers withhold rain from heaven was intimidated by a woman threatening him. He becomes so discouraged that he runs away and prays that he might die! I believe that this was more than just a woman though; this was a spiritual attack upon his life. Sometimes when we are under a spiritual attack, it can leave us feeling so discouraged that we want to give up. It can make us think that everything is useless, when in fact there is no logical reason for how we are feeling. Elijah had just come from a great victory and yet now he wants to die. When we are under attack, we need to run for the presence of God. The anointing may sometimes attract opposition from the enemy but we need to recognise it, not allow it to destroy us and to run for the presence of God to get set free. When Elijah finds the presence of God in a cave, it is here that God gives Elijah the instructions to go and anoint Elisha.

Elijah leaves the cave and goes in search of his new assignment and when he finds Elisha, he goes up to him and throws his cloak around him.

1 Kings 19 v 19 "Elijah went up to him and threw his cloak around him"

Some translations may say "threw his mantle around him". A mantle was symbolic of the anointing of God. Elisha was just in the field ploughing with the oxen, when Elijah came up to him and threw his mantle over him. Elisha realises that this is the call of God that has come to him, and he tells Elijah that after he has taken time to put things in order and say goodbye to his family, then he will follow Elijah and become his attendant. Elijah says in v 20 "Go back, what have I done to you". In other words; do what you like, I was only the messenger! Elijah does not hang around trying to persuade Elisha to follow him; he simply does what God has asked him to do and then turns to leave. However, there is something about the anointing and the presence of God that once you have tasted it, you can never settle for anything less. Maybe Elisha had been quite happy ploughing the fields, but once Elijah threw that mantle, his life was changed forever. He knew that he could never again be happy just ploughing those fields, he had to follow the call of God. Once we have experienced the presence of God and know what the call of God is for our lives, we will never be able to be satisfied with doing anything else in our lives or in living in anything less than the presence of God that we have experienced. The anointing creates a hunger in our lives for more of God's presence.

V21 "He burned the ploughing equipment to cook the meat and gave it to the people and they ate. Then he set out to follow Elijah and become his attendant"

He totally burned his old life in order to follow his new life. He burned his bridges, there was no going back. Ploughing was his livelihood - surely he could have followed Elijah and just kept the equipment in case it didn't work out? Jesus said that when we turn our hand to the plough, that we should not look back. Elisha decided that day, that he didn't want any temptation to go back to his old life, he had decided to answer the call of God. Sometimes when God calls us, he may call us to totally change the direction of our lives. For others, it may not be so radical, but for some it is. When Jesus called the fishermen as his disciples, it is interesting how they immediately dropped their nets and followed him. There is something about the voice

55

of God calling you that makes you change your life to answer the call. Elisha becomes Elijah's attendant and he walks with him and serves him.

Elijah's Mantle

I believe that we are living in a time now when the Lord is again restoring the prophetic office to the church and where the Elijah's mantle is being placed upon men and women of God. What is the Elijah's mantle in a prophetic sense of the word?

Elijah was a true prophet of God who was used by the Lord to mentor and train up the Elisha of the day. I believe that a true Elijah is one who covers other ministries and who is used by God to not only be a prophet but is also one who looks for the next prophet along the line to pass the baton on to. Every Elijah should be looking for the Elisha that they can train and pass the work on to and every Elisha should be looking for their Elijah to follow. If our work only continues for our life, then we have failed in our mission to carry on the work after we have departed this life. We need to train others to carry on with the work that we have begun. Elijah spent a number of years training up Elisha to carry on the work after he had departed to be with the Lord. Elijah was a man who carried the true prophetic voice of God and was not afraid to speak forth what the Lord was saying, even when it meant that he had to flee for his life. God is seeking to raise up those who will stand for him and declare the word of the Lord in all it's fullness to the world. He will raise up those who will speak to people in high power and influence and will change the course of time.

The Elijah mantle was a mantle of restoration - in Malachi 4 v 5 "See I will send you the prophet Elijah before that great and dreadful day of the Lord comes. He will turn the hearts of the fathers to their children, and the hearts of the children to their fathers".

Here the scripture is saying that before the day of the Lord's return, there will be an increase of the Spirit of Elijah poured out and it will be a restoration mantle. God is wanting to restore his church before his return and he is going to use the prophetic mantle again in our time.

Another mantle that I believe is coming upon the church at this time is the John the Baptist Mantle. John the Baptist was referred to as being a forerunner to prepare the way for the Lord. I believe that we are prophetically living in the days, when God is calling for the same anointing to be upon the church - where we will be a forerunner for the second coming of the Lord - to prepare the way for the Lord's return. God is looking for a clear voice that will call out in the wilderness to prepare the way for the Lord's return.

Steps to a New Anointing

1) Be Faithful in someone else's ministry

I believe that the first key to receiving the anointing of God, is that we must be prepared to be faithful in someone else's ministry before God will give us our own. The Lord told me that he had called me to preach many years ago, but I did not start immediately, I had to train and prepare and be prepared to serve others who were already doing what I wanted to do. Some of the things that we may be asked to do, may not seem as if they have any relation to our calling - but the relation that they have is called "Serving"!

Mathew 25 v 21 "You have been faithful with a few things; I will put you in charge of many things"

We need to learn to be faithful in the places that God has put us in at this time and God will bring the increase and the expansion to our ministries. God will also increase the anointing upon our lives as we are faithful to use what he has already given to us. I mentioned earlier in the book about how I began my ministry and how God has slowly led me along the years. If God started us off in a high position then most of us would not know how to handle it both in a natural sense and also spiritually as well. We have to learn things and also God is watching to see what our heart attitude is like; will we give him glory. Many who rise up quickly can end up falling because they become proud or they give in to temptations and bring the work of the Lord into dis-repute.

God wants us to stand firm until the end completing the work of the Lord not just starting the work of the Lord, therefore sometimes he seems to take us around a long way before we get to the fulfilment of all that he has promised us.

In 2 Kings 2, Elijah begins to tell Elisha that he is going to be taken away from him and that he has to visit several places before the Lord will supernaturally transport him to heaven.

2) <u>A hungry and a loyal heart</u>

2 Kings 2 v 2 "Elijah said to Elisha; stay here, the Lord has sent me to Bethel. But Elisha said "as surely as the Lord lives and as you live, I will not leave you" so they went down to Bethel"

Three times, Elijah tells Elisha that he can stay where he is because the Lord is sending him to somewhere else, but each time he insists on going with him. I believe that this shows two things about Elisha. It shows that he had a loyalty towards Elijah and refused to leave him even up until the end. We need to not only be faithful to those God has called us to serve, but we also need to be loyal. Elisha stayed close to him, until he was called away; he refused to leave his side. I believe that more than ever, leaders need to have people who they can depend upon, those who will stand with them and support them, people who they can trust - Elisha was such a man.

Also, Elisha had a hungry heart and he did not want to miss out on anything that Elijah was going to experience along the way. He reasoned in his mind that if God was sending Elijah somewhere, then he wanted to be there too. There are some people who carry the anointing of God so much on their lives, that you just love to be where they are in case you might catch some too!!

After leaving Gilgal, The next three places that God called Elijah to go to before he was taken away were; Bethel, Jericho and the Jordan. Elijah told Elisha that he could stay at Gilgal if he wanted to. Gilgal speaks of the place of new beginnings, so this could represent the place of salvation. We can stay at the place of just being saved and be content with that or we can move on to experience more of what God has for us. Many people give their lives to the Lord, but they never grow, they never progress any further in the Kingdom of God and they miss out on so much that God has for them.

The next place that Elijah was sent to was Bethel; Bethel speaks of the place of the presence of God. After Jacob had an encounter with God, he called the place "Bethel" saying - "how awesome is this place, this is none other than the house of God". Before we can experience a new anointing on our lives, we must have been to Bethel. We must have been to the place where we have experienced a fresh touch of the presence of God upon our lives and said "how awesome is this place". A fresh touch of the presence of God is an indication that we are going to a higher level of anointing in our lives.

Next they are taken to Jericho; Jericho speaks of great battles but also great victories. Jericho was where the walls came down when they marched around them for 7 days. Often we will go through a battle just before we are about to receive a new anointing on our lives, but as we march out in the power of God, we can see those walls fall.

Next they are taken to the Jordan - the Jordan speaks of the place of crossing over from the flesh to the Spirit. It was at the Jordan, that the Israelites crossed over into the Promised Land.

In order to receive a new anointing on our lives, we need to cross over from living in the flesh to living in the spirit. It also speaks of the place of the Holy Spirit - it was at the Jordan that Jesus was baptised and the Holy Spirit descended upon him. Before a new anointing, we have to have an encounter with the Holy Spirit and hear the voice of God speaking to us. When they got to the Jordan, Elijah rolled up his cloak and struck the water, making the water divide to the right and to the left and they passed over. When you get to the Jordan, the anointing will make a way for you - all obstacles will move out of your way.

At each place, Elisha was given the opportunity to remain there and to not go any further. We can stay in the place that we are at, but if we do, we will never experience all that God has for our lives. Each time, Elisha insists on moving forward with Elijah until eventually he is asked:-

V 9 "Tell me, what can be done for you before I am taken from you?"

Not until he had endured until the end, was he asked the question - "What do you want?"
Elisha replies; "Let me inherit a double portion of your spirit"

He had seen the anointing on Elijah's life and he wanted more! We often think that it is selfish to ask for a double portion; but it is not. When we realise that the anointing is not for us but for others to benefit from, then we will realise that it is in fact, selfish to not ask for more anointing. We can only give to others, what we have already received ourselves. Therefore if we have never experienced much of the anointing and the presence of God in our own lives, how can we impart that to others?

3) <u>We need spiritual eyes</u>

V10 "you have asked a difficult thing, Elijah said, yet if you see me when I am taken from you, it will be yours, otherwise not"

Elijah could not promise that Elisha would receive what he had asked, as it was up to God whether to impart it or not. He also tells him that he has asked for a difficult thing. I believe that the reason why Elijah says that it was a difficult thing is for two reasons. First of all, to carry more anointing, means to carry more responsibility on our lives. The greater the anointing on our lives, then the more the Lord will demand of us to achieve. Also when we have a greater anointing on our lives, then there may also be greater battles for us to overcome as the enemy does not like the increase of anointing. There will also be misunderstanding from those who do not understand what we are operating in.

Why did Elisha have to be able to see Elijah in order to receive what he desired? One reason, was that Elisha had to be looking up and that indicates that he was telling Elisha, that the anointing would come from God, not from him. Also the way that Elijah was taken was in a supernatural way and not everyone would have seen it. Elijah was taken up to heaven in a whirlwind and with chariots of fire and horsemen. I do not believe that these chariots were visible to the natural eye - it was a supernatural event. Chariots of fire in the bible are used to describe angels (Psalm 68 v 17, Isaiah 66 v 15) When Elijah went up to heaven, Elisha was given an open heaven experience to see angels and to encounter the supernatural realm. To anyone else around at the time, it may have just looked like Elijah suddenly disappeared. Therefore, Elijah was saying to Elisha, if you have spiritual eyes to see what is about to take place, then God has chosen you to carry this new anointing on your life. In order to walk in a new anointing, we have to have spiritual eyes to see the things that God wants us to see.

The road to the anointing is a glorious road, but it is not always an easy road. There is also no easy route to moving in the anointing. People can lay hands upon us to receive, but in order to keep that anointing flowing in our lives, we have to maintain it by spending time in the presence of the Lord or else the cutting edge of that anointing will begin to fade. We have to have spiritual eyes in order to be able to see what God wants us to see along the way.

As Elisha continues along the way, he sees Elijah go up in the whirlwind and he begins to cry out, because he realises that he is about to receive the desire of his heart. Elijah had told him that if he saw him when he left, then the anointing was his. Elisha begins to get excited as he realises that he is about to receive a double portion.

4) Throw off your old anointing

V12 "Then he took a hold of his own clothes and tore them apart"

Remember he already had a mantle, from when Elijah threw his cloak over him when he first called him. So when Elisha, tore his own clothes, he was throwing off his old anointing, in order to receive a new one. Sometimes, we only think of having to throw off those things which are not good, in order to receive from God. But when our season is changing or increasing, then we may have to throw off even those things which were once good, in order to receive something better. When we try to live in the good old days, we will never receive the good new days that God has for us. We can all look back and have memories of things that God has done or ways that he has used us or the times when we experienced his presence, but those times are gone and although we can learn from them, God has a new thing for us and we need to look forward in order to receive it. Elisha was willing to throw off his old anointing, in order to receive a new one.

5) Pick up your new anointing and use it

He then picked up the cloak that had fallen from Elijah and he went back to the Jordan and he struck the water with it. God did not drop the mantle onto Elisha's shoulders, he had to go and pick it up. We have to want the anointing in order to receive it; it will not just land on us by accident. In meetings when I speak about the anointing, I will usually ask people to come forward if they want to receive from the Lord. Yes, God can minister to people sitting in their seats, but I believe that there is something about actually getting out of your seat and being willing to come forward and indicate to the Lord that you are serious about receiving what he has for you.

Once we have received an anointing upon our lives, we have to do something with it. The anointing is for a purpose, it is not just so that we can look good, but so that we can get a job done.

Isaiah 61 v 1 "The Spirit of the sovereign Lord is upon me, because he has anointed me to preach good news"

Jesus declared that the Spirit of the Lord was upon him in order to get a job done. The anointing is given to us so that we can preach good news, heal the sick, cast out demons, raise the dead and proclaim liberty to the captives. The anointing is to be used and Elisha picked up his new mantle and he went to the Jordan to try it out. The Jordan as we saw earlier represents the place of the Holy Spirit and the place of new beginnings, the place where the voice of God is heard. To operate effectively in the anointing, we need to have a relationship with the Holy Spirit and know his voice and direction in our lives. It was the Holy Spirit who came upon Jesus at the baptism and empowered him for the task ahead. It was the Holy Spirit who raised him from dead and it is the Holy Spirit who has been left here on earth now to walk with us. One day when the Lord returns, the Holy Spirit and the church will leave together to go back home to the Father to the place being prepared for us by the Son. Right now, we are partners with the Holy Spirit in bringing good news.

After Elisha had received this double mantle upon his life, we read that he went on to have an amazing ministry of miracles and of raising people from the dead. He did not seem to suffer with the same bouts of depression that Elijah suffered with and he did double the amount of miracles that Elijah had done in his life. Elijah must have been pleased with what Elisha went on to do. He had trained him and mentored him and now he had gone on to achieve more than his mentor. There is a lesson in this too for us; if God uses us to train others; we need to be willing to release them to do even greater things than us. Sometimes, we think that because we have trained someone, that they should always be less than us - but there comes a time of releasing and if someone we have trained achieves great things, we should be pleased because we had a part to play in that. We should be honoured that God allowed us to shape their lives for a season, not be jealous that they did more than us. I believe that we will all share in the same rewards together anyway. When we bring someone to the Lord or have a part to play in their development in some way, then I believe that whatever they go on to achieve, we will receive part of that reward with them. If it was not for us, then maybe they would not have got to where they are now, so let's rejoice when people succeed who we helped at some time. God will surely not forget what we have done!

The Anointing is all that you need

2 Kings 4 is the story of the widow's oil and I believe it highlights the importance of the Anointing but also how we can underestimate the power of the anointing in our lives. This passage is the story of a lady whose husband had died and she is left in great debt and the creditors are going to come to take away her sons as slaves to pay for the debt. Her husband was a prophet and a God fearing man and so she cries out to Elisha saying that her husband revered the Lord and yet now she is about to lose everything. Elisha says to her:-

V 3 "What do you have in your house" and she replies
"Your servant has nothing here at all, except a little oil"

The answer to all her problems was in her house and yet she did not even realise it. Often the answer to our problems can be right in front of us and yet we do not recognise it. Oil speaks of the anointing of the Holy Spirit - She had the anointing in her house and yet she thought she had nothing!

Sometimes, circumstances can come against us and we can feel powerless to do anything about it, we can feel that we have nothing, just like this lady. Yet what we do not realise, is that if we have the Anointing, then we have everything that we need. The anointing has the power to overcome hurdles and to bring miracles into our lives. The power to set her free from all her problems was in her house and yet she did not realise it. When Elisha realises that she has oil in her house, he instructs her to go and ask her neighbours for lots of empty vessels and to begin to pour oil into them. As she takes those empty vessels, she begins to pour and pour and pour and pour and a miracle begins to take place. That small pot of oil increases and does not run dry until there are no more vessels left to pour into. As long as we are using the anointing and have somewhere to pour it, it will keep on flowing. Only when the vessels ran out, did the oil stop flowing. There is a saying "If you don't use it, you will lose it". As long as we are using the anointing, it will keep flowing and increasing, only when we no longer need to use it will it stop flowing. Such an amazing miracle happened that day, not only was there enough oil to sell to pay off her debts, but Elisha also tells her that she can live on what is left. This was no small amount of oil! Enough to pay her debts and to have enough money left to live on! God is more than enough, he is the abundance God, and it all came from the un-seen anointing in her house.

What do you have?? We often don't realise what we have. When God called Moses, he asked him "What is in your hand?". Moses thought that he didn't have anything to serve God with, but God said that whatever he had, he would anoint, so that Moses could perform miracles with it. We may not think that we are much or that we have much, but God just wants to know "What do you have?" and "Can I use what you have?". God wants to breathe life into what we have and make it an instrument of supernatural power in his hands.

If we are facing a difficult situation, then all we need is in the anointing. If we want to step out in faith and serve God, but we feel afraid - then all we need is in the anointing. As we step out and begin to release the anointing, it will keep pouring and multiplying in our lives.

Serving the anointing - The Prophets Reward

2 Kings 4 v 8-37 is the story of the Shunammite woman and her son who was raised to life by Elisha. Elisha was a travelling preacher and as such often needed to have different places to stay. Elisha used to pass by near to the Shunammite woman's house quite often and so she decided to make up a little room for him, so that he could stay whenever he came that way. I believe that what this lady saw was the anointing of God upon Elisha's life and so in effect, when she welcomed Elisha into her home, she was also inviting the anointing into her home and life. Later on, we will see that she received a great reward for welcoming the anointing into her home and for receiving the anointing on Elisha's life. Elisha often used to stay with this lady and her husband and one day, he decides to ask her what she would like in return for her kindness. He finds out that she desperately wants a child and was not able to have one, so he prophesies that she will have a child by the same time next year. She finds this hard to believe but it turns out exactly how Elisha prophesied it to be. However, some time later, the boy becomes ill and dies, yet the first person she goes to find is Elisha. She reasoned that Elisha had prophesied life once, so he could do it again. As Elisha comes to the house, he breathes over the boy and life returns to him - he is raised from the dead.

The story continues in 2 Kings 8 where we read that the woman had been instructed by Elisha to go and live in another land for a while because there was going to be a famine in the land. Serving the anointing will save you from times of famine, even when those around you are experiencing a famine, there will be abundance in your house. At the end of the 7 years of famine, she goes back to her original land to ask the King for her house and land back. She just happens to arrive at the King's palace just as Gehazi, Elisha's servant is talking to the King about her and her situation. What a co-incidence! And yet God is not into co-incidences, he is into God incidences. God had set up the meeting, so that when the lady arrived, she would already have favour with the King. The King instructs his official concerning her:-

V6 "Give back to her everything that belonged to her, including all the income from her land from the day she left the country until now"

She not only received back what she had originally, but she also got back everything from the time she left until the time she returned. In others words, she got back with interest. I want you to think for a minute about what would have happened if that lady had not invited Elisha into her home. She may never have received the son that she so desperately wanted and she also would have had no warning or protection from the famine - but instead she received a son and she was taken care of through the famine. I believe that she received a prophets reward. By welcoming a prophet of God into her home, she received a prophets reward from God which was the desire of her heart, protection and restoration. Even when the enemy tried to steal back her promise, God restored the boy back to her and in the end she ended up with more than what she had left behind.

I believe that when we serve those who have the anointing of God on their lives, there will come a special blessing into our lives. God will do something for us that money can not buy and God will take care of us in the midst of the famines of life. We need to ask the Lord for ways to bless people who are anointed, but not because we want something from them, but just because it is a privilege to serve them. The heart should not be "what can I get from them", but "What can I give to them". The blessing is simply a by-product from that but should not be our main motive. People can often tell if you are hanging around them to get something or if you are genuinely there to serve them.

CHAPTER 4

ENTERING THE HOLY OF HOLIES
THE GREATEST KEY TO THE ANOINTING

I believe that the greatest key to moving in the anointing is an intimate relationship with God and the ability to enter into the presence of God in our own personal lives and not just when we are in church. The depth of our anointing will be according to the depth of our relationship. When you have spent time with God, then as you enter into a public meeting, the overflow will naturally take place. What you store up in the secret place, will pour out in the public place.

In the Old Testament, the Israelites had a portable place of worship called a "tabernacle" which was a tent of meeting. God gave Moses specific instructions for the setting up of the tabernacle, with the three sections of the outer court, the inner court and the most holy place (Exodus 25 v 8-9). The priests were to perform their duties in the tabernacle, to minister before the Lord and to make atonement for the people. Everything in the tabernacle was to be sprinkled with blood and kept pure (Lev 16 v 14). Only the High Priest was allowed into the Most Holy Place or the Holy of Holies and then only once a year and never without blood to make atonement for his own sins and then for the sins of the people (Lev 16 v 2). It was in this place that the Shekinah Glory would fall and God would meet with the High Priest and give him all the instructions for the people (Ex 25 v 22). Entering the Holy of Holies was a solemn occasion and was done with much fear and trembling in case God should strike him down with his awesome presence (Ex 28 v 34-35). The high Priest even had to wear bells around the hem of his garment as he went in so that as long as the bells were ringing, the people waiting outside knew that the priest was still alive! What a privilege we have today when through the cross, the curtain of the temple has been torn in two and access to the very presence and glory of God has been opened up to every believer (Mathew 27 v 51). As we enter into the glory of God, we come out with the radiance of the Lord and carry his glory to the nations with fresh revelation from the throne room of God.

Many times, I have experienced the awesome presence of the glory of God filling a meeting to the point where I have stood and watched God doing miracles in front of my eyes. One meeting that I was in; the glory of God began to fall in the meeting and as we stood in his presence, I was watching the Holy Spirit ministering to peoples lives. Then one lady who had come to the meeting on crutches suddenly announced that she had been completely healed as she was just standing in the presence of God! We had entered the Holy of Holies and in that place, there is healing. Several times in Africa recently, the Lord has led me to set up a illustration of the tabernacle and invite the people to walk through into the Holy of Holies. It has an awesome privilege as I stood and watched God moving and touching peoples lives. I watched as people were being delivered as they entered into the section set up as the Holy of Holies. Demons were being cast out - not by a person - but by the presence of God - a glorious sight to see. Ministering in the glory goes beyond the anointing - the anointing is us looking good but the glory is God taking over to minister himself!

Another lady had come to the meeting and she was in a desperate state - in fact she had told God that if he didn't do something in her life, then she would end her life that very night. As she came into the meeting, I was teaching on the tabernacle and the presence of God. Then I invited the people to come forward and walk through the tabernacle that I had made up with chairs and props on the stage. Later, this lady came to testify that as she walked through the chairs and came to the section of the Holy of Holies, that she felt a big burden lift off of her and when she returned home, she had been totally delivered from wanting to end her life! Praise God! Just one touch from the King changes everything. We can try to preach, we can try to minister but just one moment in the presence of the Lord changes everything in someone's life. Let us get to the place where we surrender and allow the Lord to use us however he wants and if at times, that means just getting out of the way and allowing him total free reign, then we are willing to do that.

Another time, I was ministering and I was telling a testimony about a lady who had been healed from deafness; as I was sharing this testimony another lady said that she could feel faith rising up inside of her. She had been suffering with hearing problems for 30 years and yet that night faith was rising within her. When it was time for the ministry, she came forward and announced "I know that I am going to be healed tonight". I turned to her and said "according to your faith, be it unto you". As I placed my hands on her, the power of God came upon her and not only did she receive total healing for her hearing but she then discovered that all the pain in her body had disappeared as well! God is good!

The three sections in the tabernacle, represent the three journeys of our Christian life. The outer court was where the altar of sacrifice and the laver were; representing the place of salvation. It was the place where the animal sacrifices were made and then the priests would wash themselves in the big bronze washing bowl called a laver (Ex 30 v 17-21). Here in the outer court, we see a prophetic picture of Jesus who would become our sacrifice - without sacrifice we can not enter any further into the presence of God. As they washed in the bowl which was made up of mirrors; it represented washing with the word and also water baptism. It is interesting that the bowl was made of mirrors because as they washed, they had to see themselves (Ex 38 v 8). When we come to the Lord and allow him to wash us; we have to see ourselves before he can truly cleanse us of all un-righteousness. The entrance into this first section was called "The way". Then in the second section was the place called the Holy Place and in this section there was the lamp stand and the bread of the presence and the altar of incense. The Priest had to make sure that the oil in the lamps were kept continually burning before the Lord (Ex 27 v 20) and the bread of the presence was fresh before the Lord (Ex 25 v 30). The lamp stand represents the Holy Spirit and the oil that is to be forever burning in our lives - it represents baptism in the Holy Spirit and fresh revelation in our lives. The bread of the presence is the fresh manna from heaven - the word living in our lives every day. It also represents communion and the body of the Lord that was broken for us. Then on the altar of incense the Priest had to offer up much incense before the Lord to make a smoke screen for him to enter beyond the veil into the Holy of Holies. In Revelation 8 v 3 it speaks of the prayers of the saints being like incense before the Lord. The entrance to this second section was called "truth". In this second section we see a picture of the second part of the Christian journey where we have gone beyond the experience of salvation and now we have experienced the baptism in the Holy Spirit. We know the revelation of the Spirit, we receive fresh manna from heaven and we know how to pray and to worship before the throne of God. Let me say, that I believe that most Christians stop at this point because they think that is all that there is to experience. But through the cross, the veil has been torn and the way has been opened up for every believer to go further and enter into the Holy of Holies - the place of the glory of God behind the curtain (Hebrews 10 v 19). The place where only the high priest could enter, is now open for everyone. The name of the veil or the curtain was called "life". Behind the curtain in the Holy of Holies was were the ark of the covenant was - the symbol of the glory of God. Many times, the Israelites carried the ark from place to place and wherever it was, they had victory and then one time when the ark was captured, the people cried out "Ichabod" which means "the glory has departed" (1 Samuel 4 v 21). It is very sad that today in many churches there is "Ichabod", the glory has departed a long time ago and yet the saddest thing is that in some of those places, they continue church as normal not even aware that God's presence has left.

When Jesus declared; "I am the way, the truth and the life" he was declaring that he himself was the way into the glory of God. It is time for the glory of God to be restored to the church. King David was a man who determined to restore the ark - let us be people with a mission to restore the ark of God to its rightful

77

place.

It was very upsetting when I did the tabernacle illustration at one place in Africa and I watched as the people approached the place representing the curtain. Most people stayed in front of the curtain and there was much crying and repenting and striving that was taking place. It seemed that they were struggling to go beyond that point; maybe they did not feel worthy or they were afraid. As I stood watching this; I was praying "come on, you can go beyond the veil". Eventually one by one most of them moved past the curtain and into a new experience with the Lord. Of course it is right to repent and be reverent before the Lord but God has also called us into his glorious freedom - we are children of God - heirs of salvation. Children do not stand on ceremony, they just enjoy! We have been called to enjoy the presence of God that has been opened up to us - we can not earn our way in, the price has already been paid.

When the High Priest went in to perform his duties, he had to put on the sacred linen garments but when he had finished his duties, he was told to take off the linen garments and leave them there and to put on his regular clothes to come out to the people (Lev 16 v 23-24). When Jesus rose from the dead and the disciples went to the empty tomb they found the strips of linen lying there (John 20 v 5-7). He became our High Priest and was now showing that "it is finished". He had finished his priestly duties and he left the linen garments in the tomb as a sign to the disciples that he had finished. The way into the Holy of Holies is now open! Let us enter with confidence.

As we enter into this new dimension, we will begin to see amazing things happening as the glory flows out from us as we minister to others. Why did Peters shadow heal the sick? Because he had glory coming from him. I believe that it is time to move up another level to an anointing of glory; where we can change atmospheres and people will be healed and set free just in his presence that we carry. I believe that the Lord is calling us to be "Glory carriers". In the Old Testament the Priests had to carry the ark of the covenant on poles ahead of the people. Several times, people were struck down dead because they dared to touch the ark in an inappropriate way. They had not learnt how to carry the glory of God. In these new days, God is looking for men and women who will know how to handle and carry the glory of God.

The Anointing Oil

Exodus 30 - In this passage of scripture we read of the five main ingredients that Moses was instructed to include in the sacred anointing oil to be used by the priests. I believe that there is a great significance in the five ingredients that were to be used and we can learn a lot about the anointing by looking at what these were.

The Ingredients used in the anointing oil were;

Liquid Myrrh

Myrrh was an expensive ancient oil that was a gum resin from a small shrub like tree. It was a bitter plant from which sweetness was obtained only after bruising. I believe that we see a connection here between the bitterness of the cross of Jesus, but out of it came the sweet victory and from where we can receive the anointing. Everything that we have comes through the bitterness of the suffering at the cross. I believe that this also has another meaning as well. If we want to walk effectively in the anointing, then we will need to die to our fleshly desires and walk in the Spirit. Also, it is also as we have been through trials and situations, that we are able to come out of them with the sweet smell of the anointing of God upon our lives. I believe that anyone with an effective ministry, has been through some kind of situation in their lives where they have needed to depend upon God and where they have had to seek the face of God; where they have been through a trial, but come out with a testimony. Even Jesus went into the wilderness but when he came out, he was in the power of the Holy Spirit.

Myrrh also had healing properties - in Mark 15 v 23 Myrrh was offered to Jesus on the cross to dull his pain, although he rejected to take it. In the anointing there is healing in every form. When the anointing is present, there will be healing that will take place, both physical and emotional.

Myrrh was also used to embalm the dead. This is symbolic of preservation. I believe that the anointing upon our lives has the ability to preserve us. The anointing will keep us strong, healthy and looking young.

Myrrh was also burned to repel insects! When the anointing of

God is upon your life, it will keep the bugs away! In other words, the anointing of God will keep the enemy away from your life because of the power of God that is upon you.

Myrrh was also used on the doorposts of a new bride and groom (Song of Songs 5 v 5). This indicates that myrrh was associated with intimacy. The Bible tells us that the church is the bride of Christ and the anointing will bring us into a place of intimacy with the Lord.

2. Fragrant Cinnamon

Cinnamon bark was used for flavouring, a medicine and is a stimulant - it has a warm pleasing and peculiar smell. The anointing will bring flavour into our lives and will energize us with the power of God. The Bible speaks about us being a sweet smelling aroma to the Lord and to those around us. When the anointing is upon our lives, we will be different and will be the salt and light to the earth that God intended us to be.

3. Fragrant Cane

Fragrant cane grows in India and Arabia and the root word means to "stand upright". The more that the bark is beaten, the sweeter the fragrance becomes. The anointing will enable us to stand upright in the midst of trials and to emit a fragrance of the Lord. It is also true that when persecution comes to the church, then the church shines more brightly and more of the anointing is seen upon their lives.

4. Cassia

The fourth spice to be used was cassia which was used for flavouring and medicine. The aromatic bark comes from a shrub which grows only on heights of around 8,000 feet and flourishes where other plants can not grow. The anointing will enable us to live our lives at a higher level in the spirit and to rise up on those wings like eagles.

5. Olive oil

The last ingredient included in the anointing oil, was olive oil itself. Oil represents the Holy Spirit without whom there is no anointing! Oil was used to heal and to energise as well as to aid in giving light and fire. The anointing will heal us and energise us and will help us to see the way that we should go and to give us vision for our lives as well as putting the fire of God into our hearts and lives. In the parable of the ten virgins, five of them were wise with their lamps ready with oil, but five were foolish and did not have any oil for their lamps. When the bridegroom returned, the wise virgins were ready to meet him for their lamps were burning brightly, but the foolish ones were left panicking as to where to buy oil for their lamps. Unfortunately before they were able to locate the oil for their lamps, the bridegroom had left without them. We all need to make sure that we are constantly filled with the oil of the Holy Spirit and not be caught out oil-less!!!

FAVOUR WITH THE KING

When we have favour with the King, then doors will open before us. Esther was one lady who changed the destiny of a whole nation because she was willing to go before the King to plead for her people. Are we willing to enter the throne room of God to save the people who are perishing? Esther was chosen to be queen after she had completed 12 months of beauty treatments (probably including some of the ingredients listed above). As we allow the Lord to cleanse us, he is making us ready for his throne room. All we need is one word from the King and everything changes. The door to heaven is standing open before us (Rev 4 v 1-2) and the Lord says "come up here and I will show you". All through the Old Testament, the prophets cried out for the Lord to "come down" but Jesus has come down, he has defeated all the powers of darkness at the cross and now he has ascended and he is calling us to "come up higher" come up to his presence, come up to his throne room and in that place, he is extending favour to us and giving us revelation.

To operate in the anointing, we must come up higher. Just like Elisha had to be able to see into the supernatural realm to receive the double portion, so we must be people who are looking up higher, coming up higher, living in a higher level. As we are living in these end times, we need to be ready for the supernatural things that the Lord wants to do in and through us. Whenever we begin to talk about the supernatural, we have one of two reactions; either an un-healthy interest or a stepping away completely. In this nation, often the supernatural and the church are not thought of in the same sentence. Because we are sometimes afraid of the wrong supernatural, we have backed away from the real supernatural. I believe that everything that the devil has and does is only a counterfeit of the true power of God. God is wanting to restore the true power of God to the church that the world may see that Jesus is alive.

CHAPTER 5

UNDERSTANDING YOUR CALLING

Ephesians 2 v 10 "We are God's workmanship created to do good works, which God prepared in advance for us to do"

We have been created with a purpose in mind, God has something for everyone of us to do. So many people ask me "what is my calling, what does God want me to do?". I believe that the reason why we are on this earth is because there is something for each one of us to accomplish before we go home to heaven. The word "workmanship" simply means - something that is created with a purpose in mind. So when God created you he made you perfect for what he was wanting you to fulfil.

Jeremiah 1 v 5 God said to Jeremiah that even before he was formed in his mothers womb that he knew him and he set him apart and he appointed him as a prophet to the nations.

The call of God was on his life even before he was born! Each one of us, even when we were in our mothers womb, God knew us (Psalm 139) and he set us apart and he appointed us for the task that he was moulding and shaping us for. Therefore we are not going through life aimlessly and wondering what we should be doing - we have been created with a purpose. Our task is to seek God to find out what that purpose is and then seek the anointing to be able to fulfil it.

God has called us the body of Christ with many members each

85

operating in a different function. When we realise this and fit into our place within the body, then everything will begin to operate effectively(1 Corinthians 12 v 12-29). Imagine in a natural body if we had 10 mouths and only 1 ear! How strange that would look. The same is true in the body of Christ, he has given gifts to each one just as he determined so that together we will function properly. (1 Corinthians 12 v 4 says that there are different kind of gifts but the same spirit). We do not need to be jealous of someone else's ministry because we have our own unique to us. V 27 says that each one is part of the body. God has appointed the 5 fold ministry of the apostle, prophet, pastor, evangelist and teacher but he has also given gifts of administration all listed in the same place in v 28-29. An apostle is no good without an administrator! And one is no greater than the other, they are just different callings according to our abilities. There are some things that I am good at that others can not do but in the same way there are some people who are good at things that I would be hopeless at. Therefore we need to honour one another's gifs and work together to enhance and extend the Kingdom. I have a good friend of mine who has a great gift of hospitality - if 20 people arrived un-announced at her door, she would have a meal made up in no time at all and making it look as if it was very easy. I remember once I said to her "this is amazing", to which she replied "oh, don't be silly, anyone can do it" and I thought "no, they couldn't"! You see, because that is her gift, it seems easy to her. But then she said to me "but I couldn't get up and preach like you" but to me I find that easy because it is my gift. So you see, we all have different gifts and if we are operating under the anointing then that gift will flow with ease and we will not find serving the Lord burdensome and difficult but a joy and a delight. So how can we know what our calling is? Some people don't know their calling and want to know; others do know but are wanting to know; how can I begin or expand my calling? We will look at a few of these areas now.

The Holy Spirit will communicate

I believe that the first way that we know our calling is that the Holy Spirit will communicate it to us. John 16 v 13 says that the Holy Spirit will lead you into all truth and he will tell you what is yet to come. The Holy Spirit knows the future and he is the one who knows the plan for your life and as you seek him, he will begin to reveal that plan to you. This can occur in several ways; either through an inner witness that will not go away. You just begin to get a burning desire for a particular area - God is placing certain things on your heart. I believe that often we are the answer to our own prayers. When we begin to cry out that God would send someone to help with …. Then often the answer comes back "Go, I am sending YOU"! Next, God may confirm his call with a dream or a vision or a prophetic word from someone else. We need to understand that all dreams, visions or prophetic words must match up with scripture and also they usually confirm our inner witness that we already have. I believe that the greatest way that the Lord speaks to us is through the Peace of God.

The Anointing to Do Something

Then we have a realisation of an anointing to do something.

87

What do you do best when the anointing comes on you? I don't mean what do you do best in your natural abilities but what do you do best when the anointing comes on you. Although we may have natural abilities and God can certainly use them; often our main calling is actually something that we would not normally be able to do so that we have to rely on him to do it.

What do others see in you?

Then we have to think; what do others see in me? Especially other leaders around us. Do they recognise a certain anointing on our lives? God will often confirm our calling by others and also by the results that we are seeing. Where are we bearing the most fruit? Sometimes we have to be realistic that although there are timings and seasons and we may be in a season of waiting and not seeing much; however there should be some evidence that God is blessing whatever area we feel called to. If not, then we need to seek if we are in the right place or does God have something else for us to do.

How do we begin

Once we have established what we are supposed to be doing, then we need to know how to begin or to expand if we are already operating in our calling. I believe that the main part of this was covered earlier in the story of Elijah's mantle. We begin by serving and we begin by being faithful in small things. Find someone who is already operating in the anointing and start to learn from them and serve them. One day the mantle will fall on you if you follow till the end. In Zechariah 3 v 10 It says "do not despise the day of small beginnings" All things start small and from that place they grow to what God wants them to be. If we are already operating and want to expand then begin to seek God for the next step. Often God will only show you one step at a time and as you are faithful to take that one step then he shows you the next one. In our quieter times, then we can be busy doing things that are preparing us for the next stage. For example in my quieter months, I have taken time to get books written and cd's prepared so that when I have more busy times of conferences, then I have resources ready. With going to the nations, God has each time put one nation in front of me and then as I have been faithful to step through the door that he has opened, then I have found that another nation will open. God is waiting for us to take steps of faith to the next level.

Understanding Timings and Season

Sometimes we get frustrated and disappointed because we do not understand timings and seasons in our lives. God has a set time for the doors to open to us. In Acts 16 v 6-10 Paul wanted to go to Bithynia but the Spirit of Jesus would not allow him to. The door was closed. Now Paul could have become disappointed or he could have thought that this was the devil not wanting him to go to preach the gospel; but instead he had a vision during the night. He saw a man of Macedonia begging him to come over to them; so Paul concluded that the closed door was now directing him to another open door. Whenever God closes a door, it is because he has another one instead for us. Sometimes we are not ready for what God has planned for us or sometimes places are not ready for us. Therefore we need to keep in step with the Holy Spirit not rushing ahead and not dragging behind. Even in the natural there is a period of sowing and reaping and the same is true in the Spirit. When we are new in the Lord, we are so enthusiastic that we think we can save the world! But sometimes God has to restrain us for a while to prepare and train us before he can release us. Sometimes he hides us before he reveals us!

Divine Connections

I believe that our calling and destiny is always connected to people and places. Just like Elisha had to follow Elijah, so there is an Elijah for each one of us that God is placing in our lives. There are divine connections for us to make; people that are going to be part of our visions and destinies. Some of those people will mentor us and some of them will be people who will walk with us in the vision; there are also people who we also need to mentor. As we progress in our walk with the Lord, then we are to be training up people behind us to carry the baton on. There is a divine place and time just like Esther was chosen to be in the Kings palace for such a time as this. Just as Ruth chose to follow Naomi instead of choosing to go back to her own people but she clung to her mother in law in loyalty and by faith went to a land that she did not know. God honoured her faith and obedience and she married Boaz and had a son that ended up in the lineage of Jesus. This is an amazing story of God's grace because originally Ruth was a Moabite and the law had forbidden any Moabite from entering the assembly of the Lord right down to the tenth generation (Deut 23 v 30) because they had hired Balaam to pronounce a curse on the Israelites

(Numbers 22). For Ruth to end up marrying Boaz and being listed in the genealogy of David in Ruth 4 v 13-22 which of course is the line of the Messiah is amazing. It shows us that even if we have started out bad - we can end up good if we decide to follow the Lord with all our hearts.

The Gifts of the Holy Spirit

In 1 Corinthians 4 v 4-11 it lists all the gifts of the Holy Spirit that are available to the believer. In v 11 it says "he gives them to each one just as he determines." Therefore we can see that the Holy Spirit has many gifts in his possession and it is him who decides who to give them to. When we decide who to give gifts to we often choose people who we have a relationship with. We also choose the gifts according to the persons interests and needs etc and what we think they will like and what we think would be useful to them. I believe that the same is true of the Holy Spirit; as he holds these gifts in his hand he is looking to see; who is in relationship with me; who needs these gifts; who will use them wisely? Sometimes we are praying and asking for the gifts of the Spirit but we do not have a relationship with the one who has them. The Lord will not give precious gifts to people who do not have a relationship with him. The gifts are also for a purpose, they are to help us with the work of the Lord and they are to be used in a correct way and the glory is to be given back to the Lord and not for our own glory. Therefore God is looking to see who he can trust with the gifts that he wants to give to us. I believe that there are some people who seem to have an emphasis on particular gifts according to what ministry

God has called them to do; but I also believe that it is possible for us to operate in all of the gifts at different times. In fact, there are times, when you may need to operate in several gifts just for one situation. For example if someone comes to ask for healing; you need the gift of healing but you might also need the gift of the word of knowledge to gain further in-depth understanding of what you are praying about and then you would need to be operating in the gift of faith in order to believe that your prayer is going to work! Therefore in just one ministry instance, you have operated in 3 of the spiritual gifts. In 1 Corinthians 14 v 1 it tells us to "eager desire the spiritual gifts" but also in 1 Corinthians 13 it speaks about how love must be at the root of all that we do. If we have faith that can move mountains but have no love then we are nothing (v2). All spiritual gifts are given for the building up of the body of Christ and for us to be more effective in the work of the Lord and the motive and root behind all of it should be love. If we have no love and only power then we will become arrogant and proud and as it says in 1 Corinthians 13 v 1 then all we shall be is a clanging cymbal! Jesus came to show us the way of love. In Romans 5 v 8 "while we were still sinners Christ died for us". The cross was the greatest demonstration of the love of God.

SUPERNATURAL V THE COUNTERFEIT

God is a supernatural God, everything that he does is supernatural. He spoke and the whole world came into existence - there is nothing that is impossible for him. I believe that we need to be open to God using us however he wants to at any given time while at the same time always making sure that our focus is on God and not on the experience. When we seek for the experience more than for the source, then we can open ourselves up to a counterfeit experience. The devil is not a creator, he is a copier and masquerades as an angel of light (2 Cor 11 v 14). The bible speaks about false apostles and prophets and false workers of miracles that will occur in the end times (2 Thess 2 v 9-11) (2 Cor 11 v 13). We need to be people who can recognise the true anointing from the false. There may be many people who can perform miracles, but not every miracle comes from God. I often say that there can be many people who can do a miracle but not many who can bring the presence of God. Only true servants of God can bring the presence of God. For every miracle, we need to ask; did this bring glory to God, was the name of Jesus lifted higher through this?

In Acts 16 v 16-18 there was a slave girl who followed Paul and Silas as they were preaching and she seemed on the outside as if she was a follower of them and that she was even promoting their ministry as she called out "these men are servants of the Most High God and are telling you the way to be saved" and yet Paul operated in the spirit of discernment and knew in his spirit that this was a mocking spirit and not from the Spirit of God. He then became aggravated in his spirit and he turned around and said "in the name of Jesus I command you to come out of her" and immediately the evil spirit left the girl.

Sometimes people can seem as if they are saying all the right words but we have a witness in our spirits that something is not right. Right words - wrong spirit behind them.

Even when we are operating in the true anointing, we need to be careful to watch our motives as we begin to see greater things happening. There was a man in the bible called "Gehazi" who was a servant of Elisha. In 2 Kings 5 there is a man called Naaman who is healed of leprosy through Elisha's ministry. Afterwards Naaman wants to give Elisha a gift but Elisha refuses to receive the gift. Let me say that I do not think that there is anything wrong with receiving gifts if people want to bless us but on this occasion Elisha chose not to receive the gift and Naaman went on his way. Gehazi however decided to go after Naaman and make out that Elisha had changed his mind and to ask him for a gift. This blatant act of deception cost him his whole ministry. When he returned, Elisha challenged him as to where he had been and what he had been doing as God had given him supernatural in-sight into what Gehazi was up to (a hazard of working with a prophet!). Gehazi tries to deny that he has been anywhere or done anything but Elisha knows differently and declares that Naaman's leprosy will now come upon him. He is leprous and cast out - all because he saw an opportunity to gain from the anointing in a wrong way.

The bible speaks about the Christian life being like a race that an athlete competes in. We have been given a journey marked out for us (1 Corinthians 9 v 24-27) and it says that we should run in such a way as to get the prize. V 25 says that an athlete goes into strict training to get a crown that will not last but we have a crown that will last forever. When I was younger I used to be a competitive swimmer and went as far as swimming for my county and competing at national level. For many years I had to get up early in the morning to go for training sessions at the swimming pool and then I would come home and go to school and study and then back again for more training in the evening time. It was a disciplined strict training. I also had to be careful what food I was eating to make sure that my body was in the best condition that it could be. I remember that on race days, I would take time before-hand to focus my mind on the race so that I was concentrating all my efforts on the task ahead.   Paul gives the illustration of our Christian walk in a similar way; that we have to be focused on what we are doing. If an athlete was to run the race looking behind them or staring up into the crowds then they would soon lose vision and fall over. We have to keep our focus on Jesus and on the path way that we are walking on in order to win the prize. In v 27 Paul says that he beats his body to make it his slave, so that after he has preached to others, he himself will not be dis-qualified for the prize. In sports events, it is possible to put all the effort in and to get to the end of the race thinking that you have won the gold medal, only to then find out that you have been dis-qualified on some technicality. Let us not be people who spend our life preaching but then find at the end of the day that we have been let down by our character and falling into temptations that will dis-qualify us for the prize. In 1 Corinthians 10 v 12 it says "if you think you are standing firm, then watch out that you do not fall". When we know that we are weak, then we rely on God daily in our lives but if we allow ourselves to become proud, then we are at risk of falling BUT in Jude v 24 "To him who is able to keep you from falling and to present you before the glorious presence without fault and with great joy". If we keep our lives focused on Jesus then he will keep us from falling, keep us from being dis-qualified and we shall hear those words "well done, good and faithful servant" and we shall receive the crown of life.

Some of the supernatural ways that God worked in the bible are;

Miracles/raising the dead	1 Kings 17 v 17-21
Supernatural increase	Genesis 26 v 12
Angelic Visitation	Acts 10
Animals speaking	Numbers 22
Power over weather	1 Kings 17 v 1
Supernatural strength	1 Kings 18 v 46,
Judges 16 v 28-30	
Transportation in the Spirit	Acts 8 v 39-40
The Prophetic	Acts 21 v 10
Casting out demons	Math 17 v 14-18

I believe that all of these things can happen in our own lives - if they are in scripture, then God can use them now. Some of these things we do see happening frequently and other things not so frequently but we need to be open to all that the Lord wants to do especially in these end times.

INTIMACY/DEPENDANCE ON THE HOLY SPIRIT

Zechariah 4 v 6 "not by power, nor by might but by my Spirit says the Lord" .

Whenever I have the privilege to minister around the world and people ask me what is the key to the anointing - I will always reply; "It is a relationship with the Holy Spirit". Recently I has honoured to teach 90 pastors at a conference in India and on the last session, I said to them "If I could only tell you one thing, it would be this; always be dependant on the Holy Spirit". This is the key that I have found in my own life and ministry and I believe that it is the key for every believer and minister. When we try to serve God in our own strength, then we will find that it will be difficult and that also it will not be bearing much fruit. Jesus said "without me, you can do nothing". The same is true of the Holy Spirit. Without him, we can do nothing - he is the very air that we breathe. When Jesus walked on the earth, he was totally dependant upon the Holy Spirit. It was the Holy Spirit who was there at his conception overshadowing Mary (Luke 1 v 35), it was the Holy Spirit who came upon him at his baptism (Luke 3 v 22), it was the Holy Spirit who was present for him to heal the sick (Luke 5 17) and it was the Holy Spirit who raised him from the dead (Romans 8 v 11). If Jesus needed to be so dependant on the Holy Spirit for the success of his mission, then what about us? Do we think that we can succeed without him?

Many people talk about the Holy Spirit only in terms of the power of God and the anointing and the miracles. However I believe that the key to the power of God and the anointing and the miracles is an intimate relationship with the Holy Spirit on a daily basis in our lives. The depth of the relationship that we have in our personal times with the Lord will be the extent to which his presence shows up in a public meeting.

We need to not only have a deep relationship with the Holy Spirit but to also be dependant upon him in all that we do. I believe that this is why the Lord often calls us to do something that we can't do - so that we have to rely upon his strength and anointing and not our own.

I pray that as you have read this book that you have been challenged to seek God for more in your own life and ministry. Whatever the call of God upon your life; whether you are called to the nations or if you called to your own local area, as you are faithful in that then one day you will hear those words "well done good and faithful servant". The Anointing is for all believers - step out and ask for an increase today.

If you have been blessed by this book then please visit our website at; womenariseministries.net for more information on our ministry and how you can be involved in partnering with us and attending some of our meetings.